Not Quite a Teacher

Also available from Continuum

The Behaviour Guru, Tom Bennett
The Ultimate Teaching Manual, Gererd Dixie
How to Survive Your First Year in Teaching: 2nd Edition, Sue Cowley

Not Quite a Teacher

*Target practice for
beginning teachers*

TOM BENNETT

continuum

Continuum International Publishing Group

The Tower Building	80 Maiden Lane
11 York Road	Suite 704
London	New York
SE1 7NX	NY 10038

www.continuumbooks.com

British Library Cataloguing-in-Publication Data
A catalogue record for this book is available from the British Library.

ISBN: 978-1-4411-2096-0 (paperback)

Library of Congress Cataloging-in-Publication Data
Bennett, Tom, 1971–
    Not quite a teacher : target practice for beginning teachers / Tom Bennett.
        p. cm.
    Includes index.
    ISBN 978–1–4411–2096–0
  1. Student teaching–Great Britain–Handbooks, manuals, etc. I. Title.
    LB2157.G7B47 2011
    370.71′141–dc22
                                2010041667

Typeset by Fakenham Photosetting Ltd, Fakenham, Norfolk
Printed and bound in India

Dedication

This book is dedicated to everyone I met who cared about education, and taught me lessons I would never forget.

To Leslie Prior, Janet Orchard, George Wrigley, Lesley Swarbrick, Eugene Battini, Judith Bentley, Tom Metcalfe, Michael Evans, Justin Childs, Joe Dawson, Rebecca Gurnham, Fiona Grant, Christine Julian, Louise Northey, Jennifer Head, Shelley Wild, Rufus Sanders, Sara Kilani, Liz Smith, Michael Gillen, Martin Murray, Feroze Antia, Brian Samways, Sophie Lovett, Ben Coburn, Melanie Taylor, Evan Jones, Emily Somerville and Katalina Watt, Philip Woollett, Yassin Idrissi, Naomi and Patrick Smart, Marc James, Charlie Cohen, Morgan and Niall French, Alice Latham, Debbie Lantsbury, Bill Wynne, George Christofi, Jack Wilson, Josie Wilson, Kayleigh Fontaine, Linley Riley, Susan Boe, Toni Griffin, Kirsty Watt, William Clark, Chloe Leak and Alex Dolan.

Also to my parents, Tam and Betty, my brother Anthony, and to Anna.

Contents

Introduction

This is an NQT guide in disguise.

If teaching is a battlefield then this book describes the tour of duty, except that not only does Charlie not surf, he also doesn't put his hand up to ask a question. On the premise that watching people fall over and hurt themselves is the quintessence of comedy, this book will take you through every mantrap and pratfall that your training years will tenderly send you. I will show you my bruises and tattoos so that you know how not to get them. I will translate every acronym and portmanteau the panjandrums of education feel we can't live without. I will teach you the barely literate dialects of contemporary urban slang, then tell you why you must never use it. I will tell you which mug to buy, and where your biggest worries will come from. Then I will abandon you and never call, except when I want something. Like OfSTED.

However you enter the profession, your first two years of teacher training will be one of the biggest challenges in your life; it requires guts, stamina and levels of resourcefulness normally associated with storming a Nazi castle. On top of that is the sad fact that many teacher trainees still enter education full of anachronistic illusions about what schools are like these days. This is compounded by a training system that, with the best will in the world, often leaves beginning teachers under-prepared for the challenges of poor behaviour and disrespect prevalent in the contemporary state school.

Another challenge you will face is that the rulers of education, though well meaning, often seem to be the people least suitable to administer and guide the practice of learning in this or any other country. Formal teacher training in the UK is perversely weighted towards fashionable, questionable ideologies of learning and teaching of nebulous provenance. Bureaucrats have crept into every classroom, and the new teacher can feel strangled by the paperwork and the box-ticking.

These are my observations after teaching, training and advising new teachers from all over the UK on *The Times Educational Supplement* online behaviour forum. Fear not: teaching is still one of the most rewarding jobs in the world, despite these impediments. It is an honour and an enormous responsibility to stand before a class of children and say 'I am here to guide you.' The personal reimbursement from such a role is only matched by the tenacity and effort required to make the role work. Make no mistake: this is a hard job. And I have never been happier.

This book approaches teacher training a little differently from most other guides: I have briefly recounted my own experiences in teaching in order to provide you with some context and a sense of narrative to the challenges and hurdles in teaching that can seem vague and insubstantial until you've actually encountered them. I've tried to keep it as relevant and general as possible, although I can't guarantee I won't go off track occasionally, like an old drunk. Interspersed with these stories I've provided advice from an older, wiser self: what I should have done, and comments that illuminate the experience. It becomes a 'how-to' guide using my own history as a laboratory beagle. I suspect I don't come out of it showered in glory.

This is a map of a minefield. It's worth every step.

Good luck.

1 | The Starter

1 | No one forgets their first teacher: *Stepping on to the rollercoaster*

First steps to becoming a teacher

If you're reading this book, or you're just flicking through it in the bookshop,[1] then chances are you're already on the application rollercoaster, or you're on the next ride completely. I will refrain from entirely teaching you to suck eggs. It might be useful for some people to know a little bit more about the process, though, and the different avenues into and requirements of teaching in case you want to re-evaluate you own route; not all of them are obvious, and one of them might be more suitable for you.

Your first port of call should be the Training and Development Agency for Schools (TDA). In 2012 the TDA's functions are transferred into the Department for Eduction. They sport a rather dandy website that contains everything you need to guide you through the application process. And, unlike many websites, it celebrates form and function. They don't sponsor me or anything; it's just nice to be able to recommend a website that actually assists your research and application, rather than high-fiving itself at how oblique and impenetrable it can be.

The following applies principally to those applying to be teachers in England and Wales; if you're applying to teach in Scotland or schools in Northern Ireland, you'll need to contact their respective organizations (listed in the Appendix at the end of this book).

Every teacher in the state sector must have obtained Qualified Teacher Status (QTS); in order to achieve this they must first undergo Initial Teacher Training (ITT) which is provided in a variety of ways.

In 2003 I decided to become a teacher. For the previous ten years I had worked in bars and nightclubs in Soho, London, which perhaps didn't provide the most obvious springboard to diving into a classroom, but there

---

[1] Shame on you. I suspect the person behind the checkout fancies you. Why not approach them, using this book as a simple conversational gambit?

you go. We all have our stories, and that's mine. The first step was to register with the Training and Development Agency for Schools, or the TDA.[2] *I deliberately use the acronym because as I was to find over the next few years, everyone in education speaks in code.*

Finally I got through to the last one on my list; I was in.[3]

The language of schools

It appears that government policy is to take any loosely-connected words that refer to something remotely useful, and put them through a syntactic mincing machine before top-slicing the first letters to form another word which nobody can remember to what it refers. Throughout this book I have tried to avoid jargon, or whenever this is impossible, I've tried to slip it in slowly and gently, so nobody gets frightened. But an unavoidable impasse in this project is that the language of teaching is highly esoteric and cultish. Since the late eighties, many segments of public life and the public sector have been subtly transformed to fit a new language paradigm: the market place.

Acronyms (particularly Three-Letter-Acronyms or TLAs for short) are a Shibboleth, the Judaic equivalent of a password. In the Book of Judges, the Gileadites used to ask refugees to say the word Shibboleth in order to identify them as enemy Ephraimites. Pronouncing the word meant using the 'sh' sound, which the Ephraimites found impossible (think of a Frenchman trying to say 'thirteenth'). Those who failed felt the sword. In education, those who don't use TLAs fail to get on to the PGCE, far less become an NQT. And you can forget SLT (Student Leadership Team).[4]

These Frankenstein words are as common in the literature of education as they are in every other branch of bureaucracy/the occult, and they serve exactly the same purpose: to confuse; to obfuscate; to deter; to complicate.

This phenomenon is easy to spot: pupils and parents are often referred to as stakeholders (or more terrifyingly, sometimes as

---

[2] Or the TTA as it was then.
[3] Schools play host to a constant stream of strangers, observers and nosey parkers. Do not think for a second that you are intruding, or that you are unusual. It would be more unusual to have a day where people with clipboards were *not* wandering into classrooms at random.
[4] Strictly speaking these are initialisms, not acronyms; I asked an English teacher.

'customers', although that's a step too far for many, even if the reality reflects this usage); teachers 'deliver' education (the verb 'to teach' apparently having been made redundant); choice, transparency and student voice enjoy high profiles; and of course, targets, monitoring and data, so beloved of heavy industry, are now driving forces in the teaching community. I will put this to one side for a minute (mainly because it's evil and makes me feel like I need to wash my hands and offer something burnt to Baal), only to say that this is a language you will hear in schools a great deal, and if you want to understand what's going on around you in education, you'd better familiarize yourself with the language of economics.

Learn the language of the profession as much as you can, and you will be able to communicate in gobbledygook with teachers from all over the country, like some kind of corduroy Esperanto. Bonŝancon!

And then there was the application form. I spent a reasonable part of my life that month online, attempting to discover where I sent my John Hancock. This sounds like a walk in the park, until you consider that this was 2002, and the internet was not the internet then. Back then broadband was being hatched in a laboratory in Osaka by red-faced sociopaths who wore Sailor Moon outfits and who would later die through starvation and poor hygiene while gaming online.[5]

Not in 2002. In 2002 I had to jump start my modem (remember them? They used to live outside your computer, like a granny annexe) using a hand crank and a kick pedal. In 2002 you could see the screen load line by line, and could reliably nip out for a cup of tea while the pictures magically appeared. In 2002 if you clicked on the wrong link you had to phone the babysitter and tell them you'd be late home. So while the online option was undoubtedly a cause to rejoice in the bowels of the TTA, it offered as much convenience to the applicant as a microwave with the dial inside. Hours it took, hours; thoughtfully, there was a saving mechanism (you just know something's going to take a while when they reckon you'll have to save half way. Even an online mortgage application doesn't suggest it). And it took 'thorough' to new and previously unimaginable levels; by the time they were enquiring abut the circumference of my duodenum I was starting to suspect that nobody needed to know that kind of detail.[6]

---

[5] Usually to be found with an orange stuffed in their gobs. Fact.

[6] They don't. They're just warming up for the fall of democracy and the New World Order, when Coca Cola and the American Far Right team up with the Freemasons and the Vatican to install a surveillance camera in your bathroom.

What do I need to begin with?

◆ You will need to be trained to a degree level (or equivalent, if you enter the profession from overseas) in a subject relevant to the one you want to teach. If you want to attract funding, you will need to have at least a 2:2 to be eligible.

◆ Check with the TDA or the Department of Education websites to find out the current GCSE qualifications required. Usually, all entrants need to have a GCSE or equivalent in English and Maths, and for Primary School teachers, one in Science as well as you will have to be an everyman teacher, not unlike a many-handed Hindu deity.

Incidentally, do not mess about with the details on the application. They will check, seriously. The last hurdle of your acceptance involves them physically looking at your certificates and graduation scrolls. This wouldn't be a problem, except that I missed my own graduation day because I was appearing on 'Blind Date', a hideous ITV cringe-fest dating show that used to grip the nation in the nineties. So I had to go back to University and graduate, ten years after I left, the red-faced shame

There was something I else I had to consider: money. Far be it from me to bother with petty details, but for all my good intentions and ambitions, I wasn't going to get very far on the grants and bursaries offered to train. Which isn't to say they weren't generous – in those days they really were short of teachers, and when every other incentive scheme and marketing campaign had come up short, the panjandrums of education did the obvious thing and opened their purses to the possibility that man did not live on bread alone. There was a handsome bursary for all trainees, and if you couldn't live on the five grand that afforded you (in what city could you do this, apart from Mumbai?) then there was always the solace of the student loan nipple. When I went to University student loans were still controversial enough to be worth marching against; by the time I got to teaching they were comfortably assimilated into everyone's expectations. What had once been assumed as a right had made the transition to benefit and eventually luxury. Another five grand or so.

So: ten grand, plus change. Fine if you were a monk or a budgie. Not so hot if you enjoyed warmth and windows. I had spent too long luxuriating in three meals a day and soap in my dish to start sitting in a clammy bedsit with three Albanians under a swinging light bulb, eyeing each other while we wondered who would be the first to attempt cannibalism.

Routes to ITT

You can gain ITT several ways, depending on which route best meets your needs and lifestyle. You may, for instance, need to keep working as you train; or you may have the luxury of being able to train full time. Fortunately there are programmes to suit most circumstances.

Degree route
If you already possess a degree then there are several options open to you.

Graduate Teacher Program
This is an unusual route, requiring a strong personality and resilience. Perhaps you have Special Forces experience? You train as a teacher while working in a school, learning as you go along and working as a teacher from day one. The advantage is that you're earning straight away; the disadvantage is that you need to be tough, thick skinned, and a fast learner, because the kids won't cut you any slack if you're new – quite the reverse, in fact.

School Centred Initial Teacher Training (SCIIT)
This is a graduate program run by schools and normally takes at least a year, sometimes more. Participants can expect to combine study, projects and teaching, eventually leading to Qualified Teacher Status. Once uncommon, this will gradually become a routine entrance portal to teaching once the 2010 White Paper recommendations bed in, with a greater emphasis on in-school training.

Postgraduate Certificate in Education (PGCE)
Trainees spend a year (full time) training in schools sandwiched with lectures and tutorials in a Teacher Training Provider (TTP), i.e. college/university. Part time PGCEs allow you to juggle other commitments and take longer, naturally.

As mentioned, your degree should have significant content/skill overlap with the subject you want to teach; if it doesn't, there are bridging courses you can take; subject knowledge enhancement courses are available in most subjects, and in some cases there are bursaries available to cover the cost of the course, although offers like that tend to wax and wane with the moon, especially in this age of new austerity,[7] so check first.

Non-degree route
If you don't already have a degree then there are degree courses specifically designed for teacher hopefuls; candidates spend a number of years studying their chosen subject, as well as a range of subjects relevant to general education and teaching. These institutions combine ITT with degree qualification, and there is a balance between in-school and college/university based training, after which the candidate is qualified. Or you can take a degree first, and then consolidate it with the PGCE route afterwards. If you choose the latter you haven't committed yourself to teaching, and can decide much more easily to focus on your subject area if you decide against teaching as a career. The first option will focus you much more on the profession.

There will also be a few other significant influences on your training decisions:

1. **What subject do you want to teach?** You have some flexibility in your choice. My degree was Philosophy; I teach Religious Studies. Once you are teaching, there is often scope to branch out beyond your subject. You can also develop your own links with other departments once you've started, by showing interest, reading up on their subject, or even simultaneously retraining once you've started you job. Anything's possible.[8]
2. **What age group do you want to teach?** For many people this is obvious from the get-go; young adults (or so they claim)? Or toddlers up to preadolescents? The choice is yours. The latter offer emotional honesty, cuteness, mayhem, bodily fluids; the former offer body odour, emergent intelligence and the possibility of conversations, tempered with acne and relationship melodramas. If you're still struggling then I suggest you train to be a teacher in Denmark, where the training takes seven years and you learn how to deal with all age groups. Blimey.

---

[7] Unless you work in the DHSS. Swings and roundabouts, this recession. I once knew a guy who worked behind the benefits office desk – only to be sacked. Oh, the irony.
[8] I'm not saying this is a good thing, but schools often make decisions based on expediency rather than ideals. This can work in your favour. Not necessarily the children's, obviously.

3. **Want to teach in a faith school?** If you want to teach in a Catholic school, you'll need a Catholic Certificate of Teacher Training (web address in appendix 1).
4. **Independent or state school?** Private schools are largely free to set their own qualification requirements, so you might not need to have undergone ITT; but they will certainly need some substantial indication that you have the chops to teach their valuable customers, so forget about turning up to their interview with nothing but good intentions and a love of your subject.

I kept running into a scheme advertised for teachers called FastTrack (all one word, just like that, like PowerPoint, another piece of pointless grammatical grit in the oyster of language) which seemed all the rage. Poking further into it revealed that it was some kind of training program for teachers that ran parallel to the conventional training year. Successful applicants would have their careers 'fast tracked' (ah, I get it now) into middle management by some arcane process. The tagline was 'Be the inspiration – from the staffroom to the classroom.'[9]

Fasttrackers would be prematurely drilled into senior positions, and the adverts promised blue-skied vistas of schools run by flinty-eyed heroes and heroines staring purposefully down corridors approvingly, folders neatly clamped under their arms. Other photos showed successful, smiling young men and women dressed smartly – but still approachable – with scrubbed, happy teenagers in immaculate uniforms, also smiling, clearly inspired by the Aryan role models they had been blessed to be taught by.

It looked great. I wanted to inspire beautiful, scrubbed children in clean uniforms too. I wanted to be part of the team. I wanted the five grand bursary they were adding on top of regular training. I wanted the free lap top, printer and camera. I was inspired. I couldn't sign my name quickly enough.

Of course there was nothing as simple as a piece of paper to sign. It was another online application. Their website was so clean, so designed that I thought I was applying for an internship with the Tate Modern. It had a great deal of the smiling inspirational people, and adoring, perpetually delighted children who were forever on the cusp of enlightenment and life-changing brain waves, undoubtedly followed immediately by lifelong gratitude. I wanted in. If you have ever doubted the appeal of fascism, look no further. There was a new order coming, and you were with it or you were stuck in the mud of the past and threshed into pulp by the combine

---

[9] Even now, reading that makes my saddle feel a bit funny, and not in a good way.

harvester of the future. Presumably we'd be driving the combine harvester. I
persevered with another day and a half of intriguingly, pointlessly detailed
application forms, and once again threw my message in a bottle into the
ocean and waited.

The *FastTrack*/Teach First

FastTrack has been binned, mostly because it was hugely expensive
and failed miserably in its intention of drawing the brightest and
best into the education sector in order to prepare a new generation
of leaders. It cost a bomb, and only succeeded in recruiting about an
extra 500 people or so. We did get some lovely stationery though. The
reason why I mention it here is because it represents one of the many
alternative routes into teaching, and also acts as a sly commentary on
the way in which the Department for Education rolls out initiatives
and training programs. It is also a precursor to Teach First, a program
that enjoyed encouragement in the 2010 Education overhaul.

Teach First is a non-governmental organization (and registered
charity) that has some similar aims to the FastTrack project, in that it
aims to recruit, train and place high-fliers with leadership potential
and resourcefulness in challenging schools. They recruit at graduate
fairs and other events, and provide training and advice on making
a splash in difficult schools. I applaud their ambition. My concern
is that I find it difficult to see a direct correlation between academic
ability and leadership potential, and the ability to be a good teacher.
Becoming a good teacher is a craft, as I'll expand later. It takes time
and experience; these are non-negotiables, and all the potential in the
world won't let you leap frog that process. When I participated in
FastTrack, I was on paper a top-flight candidate; I nailed all the core
competencies and traits they were looking for. As you'll discover
in later chapters, I fell flat on my ass when put into a challenging
school. That's because teaching isn't about turning up to classes and
inspiring them with the power of your enthusiasm; it's about hard
work, relationships and getting your hands dirty. Nobody – nobody
– turns up and gets to teach, unless the children are unimaginably
biddable.

Also, I'm extremely wary (read: don't believe for a second) that
anyone should become a teacher to try to get to management as
quickly as possible, as if doing the teaching was simply a means
to an end, a tiresome impediment to a golden career. The kids are
our primary concern, and until you've become a good teacher, you

will never become a good leader of teachers. You might be a good business manager, but schools aren't commercial in nature. Just because they cost money and have to meet budgets doesn't mean that they are businesses. They're dream factories. Seriously.

Online applications

Fortunately the online application process has been streamlined considerably even since I applied. It's a relatively stress-free (although still detailed and lengthy) process that simply requires you to bite the bullet and get on with it. As with any job application, don't lie. I feel a bit foolish saying that, as if you needed to be told that lying is wrong. But in addition to the simple moral truism that lying is very, very bad indeed, is the factual truism that if you get caught lying about anything significant about your experience, qualifications or other significant factor, it can lead to your expulsion from a training course, the repayment of any bills accrued, and even to your dismissal from a teaching post.

Once you have completed Initial Teacher training, then you're free to get a job in a state school, where you'll proceed from being a Beginning Teacher (i.e. a complete rookie) to your induction year; three terms (one academic year) where the goal will be to achieve Newly Qualified Teacher (NQT) status through a combination of in-school training and, mostly, practicing by teaching, which involves trying to meet a specific set of statutory targets (the Core Professional Standards).

There's a joke in teaching[10] that NQT stands for Not Quite a Teacher. In one sense you bloody well aren't – formally you are; you've got the scarf and the blazer. But many teachers feel desperately unready to be in a classroom and teach children.

Unfortunately, two other groups often share your fears: the children and other teachers. The students will rejoice at your green hue, and if you work in a tougher school, they will mentally paint an enormous bullseye on your back. Even in a gentler, well-behaved school you will still be goaded by the less amenable students, who smell sport. This is, essentially, tough bananas. Even more unfair is that staff will also see you as the rookie, sometimes forgetting that they were just the same not so long ago. Fortunately there should be enough good

---

[10] Not a funny one obviously, because it's in teaching. Another reason it's not funny is because it's partially true.

eggs to tide you over the awkward, lengthy first date that comprises your NQT year. The others really should know better, but you'll just have to prove them wrong for their snooty off-handed manners.

A few bone-headed hours wasted on the net were just the beginning; after a few weeks I got the Golden Ticket to say I had got through the first round. The first round? Clearly I was competing to host the next Olympics.

Round two put petrol into the tank; we all had to report for a three-hour aptitude assessment on computers. It was timed, I might add. But if I thought the second round was extravagant, the next round put a powdered wig on and threw a masked ball for Elton John. We were invited to a weekend residential appraisal, where psychologists would assess if we had the Right Stuff. Let me repeat that: we were to stay at a hotel for two nights and role-play dozens of scenarios, observed by at least one (and sometimes two) trained professionals (who were clearly rubbing their hands with glee and praying nobody noticed the old money/rope exchange that was running rampant). I imagine they couldn't believe their luck. We ate fabulously (we always did on FastTrack events), and enjoyed cornucopias of embossed stationery to fend off starvation.

By this point of my life I was a veteran of corporate management training hospitality. I had a Black Belt in NLP (neuro-linguistic programming), which, combined with a pound-fifty, could be exchanged for the purchase of a cappuccino. The whole weekend was the easiest test of my life, and I filled my pockets with ballpoint pens and dared to believe I might have made the list of the elect.

Educational pseudo-science

Neuro-linguistic programming was a very voguish set of principles and techniques designed to 'model success by emulating the successful'. It's actually not entirely rubbish; unfortunately some of its keener devotees appear to think it makes them Jedi Knights, and believe they can tell when people are lying, control their minds and, possibly, walk on water. The brilliant Derren Brown intelligently uses some of its less flimsy principles as part of his act. Unfortunately Dr Bunsen Honeydew from the Muppets has more grasp of the scientific method than most NLP fans. Bizarrely, the CfBT (the quango paid by the government to run the FastTrack program) ate NLP up with a spoon, to their endless shame. And then they fed it to us. With your money. Thanks very much, incidentally.

Months later I got a letter that was so crisp, so beautifully high grade, so unmistakably unrecycled that it could only have come from FastTrack. A blind man could have read the embossed logo. As I realized I was in, I felt like I'd been initiated into the secret order. I waited for the handshake and the dagger.

In an odd harbinger of things to come, I realized that I had been accepted on to FastTrack, but not on to the Teacher Training course itself. So I phoned the colleges I had applied to, and they had no record of my application having been accepted. It was a lesson, which surely any reasonable man wouldn't have needed, that bureaucracy and administration were chaotic monsters of poetry and invention, and not the methodical engines of logic that you would have hoped for.

Two weeks after the final deadline had passed I was told that I had success-fully applied for the Institute of Education in London, my first choice. And I was FastTrack. I waited for doors to blow off their hinges as they opened for me.[11]

Overseas applicants

In recent years there has been a significant increase in the number of teachers from abroad working in the UK, especially since the introduction of work mobility across the EC. If you qualified to be a teacher outside the UK and inside the European Economic Area (EEA) then you can work in the UK; find a post, and the school will organize an assessment/training program to obtain QTS through one of the many routes. You are allowed to teach for up to four years as an unqualified teacher until you can get QTS. If your qualification is from outside the EEA then you will need also to show that you have certain other equivalent qualifications, such as Maths and English at GCSE. See the TDA website (appendix one) for more information.

Of course, nothing was easy. Being accepted simply meant that I had proceeded up to the second stage of this peculiarly tedious computer game of acceptability, and there would be new level bosses to batter. My offer of acceptance was conditional on a satisfactory interview with my training University. It might be a useful point here to pause and consider the degrees of difficulty I had endured to get to this stage, and that was presumably being repeated across the country in many thousands of permutations with other candidates. I imagine the SAS are less stringent.

---

[11] I am, I might add, still waiting.

The interview was polite and friendly, led by two kind academic women who asked me questions like 'Why do you want to be a teacher?' and 'Have you ever worked with children?' I answered as carefully and maturely as I could. I resisted the temptation to tell too many knock-knock jokes, but clearly tripped on the rug when they asked me what I thought was the most important attribute of the successful teacher.

'Charisma and passion for their subject,' was my, I thought, reasonable and uncontroversial answer. It's the kind of question that has a hundred answers because nobody has yet managed to glean the chemical formula for successful teaching. The guardians of my academic future looked owlishly at each other. I was told two weeks later that my entry to college would be conditional after all: two weeks shadowing teachers in a secondary school in addition to one week in a primary school. This wasn't a problem, until I learned from other applicants that every other conditional offer was made attached to one week of observation.

As a result of my faux pas, I was required to shadow a secondary teacher for two working weeks, which given that I was already working off the end of my job was no piece of cake.

Two weeks observing in a secondary school. What a kick in the pipes.

2 | Keep the door propped open: *Being a stranger in a strange land*

The first thing that strikes you in a Primary School is that you feel like you have eaten a piece of cake that has the words 'Eat Me' hand-piped in blue icing sugar.[1] Everything is so small. It is, I have to say, utterly charming to walk through a door that was designed for adults, into a world apparently crafted for elves and dwarves. Tables that barely touch your knees, and absurd little plastic chairs immaculately crafted in the style of a doll's house – the fact that they ape their adult cousins only adds to the oddness, like seeing Kylie Minogue in the flesh.[2] It looked like they were teaching the Borrowers. *A further aspect of miniaturization that adds to the delight is seeing all of those tiny wee people dressed in school uniform; all those shorts and ties, Dad-jumpers and the sort of shoes you would normally associate with the adverts in the back of the Sunday Telegraph, jostling for space with the Big Slipper and crease-free trousers. They all looked so middle-aged, so faux smart, that it was either heart-breakingly endearing or depressingly prophetic of their lives to come. It is, to be fair, one step away from putting trousers on a dog.*

Some of the children were barely past the nappy stage. I was immediately struck by the noise and emotion that characterizes the primary school. I confess a complete obliviousness to the charms of the kindergarten, so everything at this stage was novel, at least at first. Teachers here were not so much stern academics calmly imparting the wisdom of generations, but rather chicken herders, constantly swatting little people back into rooms, lines and tables. They wandered about like stunned midgets with Alzheimer's, perfectly innocent to rules, deadlines and responsibilities. They hung off chairs, swung off anything loose, and everything was interesting to them. Nothing held their eye for more than a minute, unless it itself changed and harboured novelty (see: telly). They were paradoxically slavishly compliant

---

[1] But if someone at school says it to you, make sure you write it up for the exclusion panel.

[2] And I have. It's very weird. She's like a regular pop star, but shrunk. She's actually the same size as she is on the telly.

to the demands of their captors, and simultaneously utterly without regard for the wishes of anyone else. You could see them howling with red-faced rage at some imagined injustice, and watch them forget about it as soon as a squirrel strolled past the window.

Getting the most out of the school visit

There are many things that you can do in order to maximize what you get out of the primary observation experience; most of it is applicable to any observation experience at any age level:

1. How do they behave?
   Behaviour management will always be one of your priorities (particularly at the beginning) of your teaching career, so it's wise to start looking at it immediately. What do the pupils do? What does the teacher do about it (or not do)? And what happens then?
2. What subjects do they do?
   The primary curriculum is in many ways different from the secondary diet. Some topics are obviously prioritized; literacy and numeracy, for instance. But there will also be other subjects threaded into their day – art, history, religious education, PE. How often do these happen?
3. How are they taught?
   This is a tricky one to answer when you're new to the profession, but you should be able to spot some basic ideas. Are they working separately or in groups? What do they enjoy, and what works best – and when? Do the more able children work with the less able, or are they kept separate? Is there a teaching assistant for the weaker pupils?
4. How is the school organized?
   Again, this is tricky to spot when you're new, but see what the big picture is. Do teachers work closely with each other? Is the Head available to chat, or is he/she a legendary figure seen only on Full Moons?
5. Do you enjoy being there?
   Your first observation is as much about observing you as it is about observing other people. What's your feeling about teaching? Still keen after you've wiped a few noses? Reckon you'd rather teach them once they can swear properly? You've learned something. Furious that they aren't learning the way you

would teach them? Good: you're passionate about method. It's all about you at this stage.

As I've emphasized, this period is for your benefit, not the school's; it's designed to assist your commitment to the profession, as well as providing you with a quick guide to the ways in which people teach and the ways in which smaller people learn. Ask if you can have any information about anything the school is good at – dealing with multiple languages, for example, or pastoral care. Speak to as many people as possible; many of them will be partial, but the more opinions about teaching you are exposed to the better. You can start to absorb a spectrum of educational ideas, and accrue or discard them later.

Keep a diary or a notebook; record your thoughts as you go along. If you can, write your reflections the same evening, or at least discuss your experiences with someone who is prepared to listen more than talk, and who has an endless tolerance for relentlessly detailed minutiae about classrooms. If you're not thinking about what's happened, you'll forget how it made you think and feel. So keep a diary.

I was instructed to follow a Reception class for two days, then a Year two class for one, then a Year six, so that I would see the stages of man speeded up like a BBC nature film. I should say at this point that I only had a vague idea what these 'years' were, but it was enough to realize at this point that Year one meant impossibly tiny and infantile, Year four meant basic speech and conversation of simple sentences, and Year six meant emergent psychological disorders and the beginnings of an appreciation of irony. Already I could see which end of the spectrum I would prefer.[3]

Towering over the room like a giant was the saintly Ms Rosa; with her was a species I had never encountered before – the teaching assistant. They didn't have them when I went to school. Any kid that needed 'assistance' usually spent five years outside the Head's office.

The teacher was doing a beautiful job, but it was dazzling to see how much effort she put into her small school of tiny, wriggling fish. Some of them barely looked out of the pram, and she had somehow to keep them all occupied and learning things, for God's sake. At times she was doing well to get them all facing the same way.

---

[3] Most people can place themselves easily on the primary/secondary spectrum, because most us instinctively know if we prefer working with older or younger children. Do you like sincerity and crocodile lines? Or do you prefer emotional angst and essays on Shakespeare?

One tiny elf came up and took my hand, as innocently as an angel.
She pointed at her face. 'My nose is full,' she said, dead pan.
I looked at her like she was a Martian. 'That's nice,' I said. I barely knew
which way up they went.
'She wants you to blow her nose for her,' the teacher said patiently.
'Ah, you see, I can't do that,' I said, relieved. 'She has to sort of do the
blowing herself.'
'No, she wants you to hold the tissue to her nose,' said my mentor, giving
exactly the answer I feared. It was revolting, of course. She didn't even try
to make the tissue.
Another tiny person came up to me before gym. From the pigtails and
pink PowderPuff Girls lunchbox it was clear she was some sort of little girl,
but nothing was certain. She held her arms up and kept them in the air,
waiting.
'She wants you to help her take her top off,' the teaching assistant said,
as if it were something reasonable, as opposed to career-shatteringly off
the scale of social acceptability. This was a minefield in a minefield, and if
you're beginning to get the impression that I was uncomfortable removing
the clothing of someone else's infant child of the opposite sex, then you
might be on to something. It's weird. I'd never considered this part of the
job before – in my last job if you were putting a hand on the customer
then you were usually throwing them out through the door. This felt like
I should be wearing gardener's gloves and using a pair of pliers.[4]
I took the bloody jumper off, sweating like a convict, and added it to my
list of reasons never to teach infants.

Contact policies

Here's a lovely minefield for us to waltz gaily through – physical contact with students. Most adults are (happily) uneasy about the thought of having physically to handle their pupils; the problem that arises from this is that often we overreact in our efforts to meet these high standards, and throw the baby out with the bathwater (without touching it, naturally). There are many times in teaching when physical contact is not only hard to avoid, it might actually be advisable or required.

When I was a pupil at school I remember a matronly Head of year who would stand next to me and hug my head into her bosom, stroking my hair. Honestly, I'm not making it up. These days you'd

---

[4] Which, I believe, is the current DfE advice given to new trainees.

be on a Sunday paper front pages in about a minute. Mind you, I also had a University tutor who tried to do the same thing while calling me 'his special boy', but by my twenties I had learned to smell a rat.

Just touching a pupil isn't by itself assault, nor is it battery. This is important; for years, teachers have acted like pupils are covered in a powerful contact poison. What does the law say? We have more rights as teachers than you might think. Guidelines issued by the DCSF (Department for Children, Families and Schools, as it was then) in April 2010, based on the Apprenticeship, Skills, Children and Learning Act (ASCL) 2009 stated the following:

Teachers are entitled to use 'reasonable force' to prevent a pupil doing the following:

a) Committing a criminal offence (or one that would be a criminal offence for an older person)
b) Causing damage to property
c) Causing personal injury
d) Prejudicing the maintenance of good order and discipline at the school whether during a teaching session or otherwise.

These guidelines apply to teachers, staff members or anyone authorized by the Head Teacher to be in control of pupils. The first three clauses deal with circumstances that many responsible adults would feel they should deal with anyway; the last one is perhaps surprising for many teachers. They are allowed to use reasonable force to maintain 'good order'.

What is 'reasonable force'? The law is vague, and probably rightly so: any attempt to generate an exhaustive list of circumstances will always be vulnerable to exceptional cases. 'Reasonable' is a term that will be tested on an individual case basis.

In this context, force can be used passively, e.g. standing in front of a student to prevent them entering a class; or it can be active, e.g. ushering a pupil away from a scene using a hand placed on their back ('reasonable', remember). Force used to restrain pupils would only be reasonable in extreme circumstances, like preventing a fight, or stopping a knife or a punch being thrown. So using the advice given above, reasonable force might be employed when:

- Preventing a lesson from being constantly ruined
- Stopping another pupil being injured or attacked
- Stopping a pupil from vandalizing school property

◆ Preventing a pupil from misusing school property in a way that is dangerous or destructive

Of course there are many other circumstances. It's great that we don't feel keen to jump in boots first to confront students physically; but it's not so great that most teachers are terrified of using physical contact as a responsible option to keep children safe from harm and disruption. Of course, we can never use it as a punishment, as that would fall under the Education Act of 1996, which rather frowns on us beating the insolence out of them. One interesting outcome is that schools shouldn't have 'no contact' policies – a well-meaning but ultimately counterproductive policy that reaches for clarity but ends up with little kids getting leathered by bullies while the teachers stand by, helpless.

An important proviso to this is that staff shouldn't put themselves in absurd danger in order to do these things; there is no legal requirement for staff to get involved in fights (nor should there be), and no teacher can be 'deemed to have failed in their duty of care by not using force to prevent injury if their own safety would be threatened.' And you *can* take their jumpers off. Wait until they ask.

I was amused to find that Reception Physical Education is very much just letting them do what they want to do anyway, only in a playground. Obviously word hit the streets fast that a fresh fish was in the room, because later that day a tiny-tiny little human being came up to me and stuck his undone shoe in front of me. He was the scout for the others, but I hadn't twigged on to this yet.

'What's this?' I said with feigned genial benevolence, 'An undone shoe lace? We can't have this! Someone will fall over and get a sore nose!' Oh the joy of having a clearly defined task to do that I knew for certain I could do. I may have been clueless in a classroom, but I owned shoe laces, and I gnawed on the bone of it as much as I could. 'There!' I said with a flourish, 'All done!' The pretend person scampered off, but behind him was an equally lovely and tiny girl with an equally tiny, undone shoe. 'Another one?' I said, still unable to smell the cheese in the trap. By the time I had knotted her plimsoll together, someone else had taken the place behind her, and she'd brought a friend. I started to tie them too. Gradually, like a very small zombie movie, most of the class shuffled into line (it was a very polite zombie movie) and I suddenly realized that the whole class had scented blood in the water. At the back of the line I could see the first boy whose laces I had tied. He was crouching down, and I could plainly see that he was untying his laces.

The teacher rescued me, like the old wizard in the Sorcerer's Apprentice.

She waved an enchanted hand and they dispersed like smoke, back to sand, paint and potato.

The next day I was relieved to sit in a Year two class, where the children by now had some kind of identifiable personalities, even if they were broad brushstrokes, caricatures of their future selves: the kind, loud girl; the introvert; the bully; the sexual exhibitionist; the bore; the obsessive worrier; the attention seeker.

For many of them, it was all too much. The laws of thermodynamics state that all systems degenerate into equilibrium. Order is far harder to sustain than chaos; it takes constant effort to create something, but a mess takes no effort at all. This is the first law of the classroom.[5]

Personal reflections

This is important: the comparisons you make between teaching now and your own experiences of being taught. Suffice it to say that you need to examine every assumption you've carried with you since your own schooldays, and see which ones need puncturing and which ones preserving. I would find, as a teacher later on, that everyone and their gay valet had an opinion on how you should teach kids, for the simple reason that everyone (apart from Mowgli and a handful of home-educated Brainiacs) was once a schoolkid, so they feel that makes them an expert. It does, in much the same way that owning a mobile phone makes me an expert on electromagnetic telecommunications, or being made out of atoms gives me authority to speak about quantum physics. Every bugger has an oar to stick in, including you. You, on the other hand, will have the sobering benefit of waking up, being born again in the River Jordan of the working classroom.

They were divided into different tables; around one such rectangle sat eight lovely students, well dressed, thoughtful and hard working. If you dropped a pencil they would all fall on it like they were saving their platoon from a grenade, and rush to outdo each other to help you. This was, I discovered, the Green Table. Next to it was the Orange Table. Another group of children, although a little more fractious than their more verdant friends next door. They weren't quite so hard working. They couldn't get all the questions right. They weren't quite as Green as the Green Table. The colours went on; I'll save you the march through the spectrum and take you straight to the

---

[5] Actually, the First Law of the Classroom is that you *do not talk* about the Classroom.

Purple Table. The Purple Table didn't even know what a colour was. They
sprawled over their space in joyous, unconscious defiance of the conventions
of the world. One of them cried a lot. One of them kept shouting 'My Dad's
going to kill you!!' to anyone, and no-one, in the manner of a drunk barking
at the moon. Another one ran around the class punching anyone in the nuts
that was too slow to realize he was from the Purple Table. The Purple Table
wasn't Green at all.

The Purple Table also enjoyed – was that the right word? – 90 per cent
of the teacher's attention, and 100 per cent, it seemed of the Teaching
Assistant's. She fed the inmates of the table different worksheets from
the rest of the class, or whispered simplified explanations of the teacher's
instructions to the majority. Sometimes she wrote an answer for one
of them, and most of the time she reminded them that they were in a
classroom, and could they stop hitting each other? And why don't you put
your shoes back on? It was heart-breaking work. I decided I needed to do
something.

Differentiation

Differentiation is the practice where students are given work appropriate to their ability; if you give colouring-in to a brainiac, you'll be
looking at a bored kid who switches off from your subject. Worse,
you might turn him into a troublesome pain in the ass, as he seeks to
amuse himself. Give hard work to a weak child, and they switch off
and give up, and before you know it, they've turned your worksheet
into an origami caricature of your mother. It makes sense to give
work that challenges them a bit. One way to look at it is to give them
something out of their reach, but *not by much*. That way they feel a
sense of achievement if they succeed.

Differentiation has become very popular as standard teaching
practice. Like many good ideas, it makes both intuitive and demon-
strable sense – you can practically see little lights go on in people's
eyes when they finally succeed in getting something tricky; you can
also watch those same lights flick off like candles in a hurricane
when you present a five-year-old with differential calculus. It's also
tied in with a more controversial concept in education: *personalized
learning*. This idea permeated state education in recent decades and
sought (quite nobly) to see each learner as a unique individual with
unique learning needs. This is probably true on many levels, but the
practical reality is that in a class of 25 kids, there is only so much
personalization that you'll be able to do. Which is fine, but many

teachers felt they were being unfairly judged and pilloried against a standard that was never possible to achieve. Even the architects of personalized learning felt that as a concept, it had limited use in a classroom environment. Thanks, guys. Next time just keep it to yourselves, eh?

There are lots of ways to achieve differentiation in your classroom; most of them don't involve you having to do a huge amount of work. The more you practise it, the better and easier it becomes, until you do it automatically when you plan your lessons.

Differentiation by Task

This includes the beloved, unholy triumvirate of worksheets so common in classes: one hard, one easy, and one pitched to the middle. This isn't totally wrong (there aren't many things in a class I would say were universally forbidden, except skunk and graphics heavy websites), but it triples the work you need to plan, and it does create awkwardness when kids realize they're getting different sheets from their peers ... and realization slowly dawns that you don't think they're as bright as Becky Swanston two rows away. If they think you have low expectations of them, it can crush their motivation.

Differentiation by Group

As with the purple and green tables, kids can be put together with others of similar abilities. This has the advantage of bright pupils pushing other pupils to new heights of competitive brightness; it can also leave you with groups of low-ability pupils who fail to drive each other; sometimes, but not always. It can work well as a temporary, time-based activity, although some teachers swear by it as a year-round seating plan. There are other schools of thought that suggest that more able pupils should be paired with less able pupils, so that one benefits from peer mentoring, and one benefits from the mentoring experience. My experience of it as a child was being paired off with a farting mentalist, every lesson for five years, being spat on and called a poof, so I'll let you draw your own conclusions.

Differentiation by outcome

This is when everyone is set a task which can be achieved in lots of different ways: a simple example would be 'write an essay on ...' or 'run around the pitch'. Able pupils will strive to write masterpieces or beat their fastest time. Less able children will produce work relative to their ability. I often hear this kind of differentiation being sneered at, and frankly I'm not sure why. It's a perfectly reasonable way to provide work relative to ability; just don't use it all the time.

Differentiation by process or method
This is when you give everyone a task to do, but offer them a variety of ways to achieve it. So students might be expected to research a topic, but they can do it by reading, by listening, by interview or by surfing the web (guess what the most popular choice would be?)

The better you get at this, the happier your kids are. I'm not suggesting that this is an end in itself (who said we were there to make them happy? Not I) but it's a nice by-product of good teaching, and one that can feed back into the quality of their education.

Even for his age, Mickey was tiny, a Jamaican boy who wouldn't meet your gaze if it was formally introduced at a masked ball. He was also the one who ran around and punched people in the goolies. I watched him constantly;[6] if he tried it with me, I vowed to drop kick him into the sandpit, and deal with the consequences.[7] But there was something about him that made your heart melt – despite his irritating tendency to hook people in the charlies (he was a southpaw, if you're interested), he responded sweetly to attention, and whenever he was reprimanded he would look at the floor and apologize in a way so sincere it had to come from the heart. Unfortunately, the second he had done so, a devilish smile would creep over his face and he would be off, looking for the next set of stones to rabbit-punch. The day I was there he was kept behind for detention during breaktime. Apparently this was practically standard procedure for him. I offered to monitor him so that Miss Amponsah could escape to the staffroom for teacher's heroin: coffee and biscuits.

'So why do you go around punching people?' I said. I omitted to add, 'in the charlies, you mentalist.' This was me, trying to get a kid to rationalize his behaviour. I had watched too much Dawson's Creek.[8]

---

[6] Unsurprisingly.

[7] This, and similar comments like it, are meant ironically. I say this because some people find it difficult to distinguish it from sincerity. I could just put 'irony apostrophes' around statements like this, or finish it off with ☺. But frankly I'd rather jump off something high.

[8] For anyone who missed this early-Millennial American drama series, it centred round a group of High School teenagers who were wracked with emotional dilemmas more routinely associated with characters in a Woody Allen movie, with diction to compare. Creepily, they were played by actors in their mid twenties.

'The chat'

Teachers waste a lot of time doing this, trying to get children to explain why they did something that is often emotionally inspired. You can't rationalize why you do everything, apart from saying, 'I was angry,' or, 'I was sad.' Not everything has a factual, conscious reason, especially with younger children

But little Mickey had his own answer. He stuck his bottom lip out and put his head down on one of his arms, swinging his left foot backwards and forwards.

'Momma says I'm a bad seed,' he said simply. I felt something cold inside me go crack. 'Momma says I got the devil inside me and I'm's a bad seed.' He said it like it was obviously true. This kid, barely six, and he described himself as having the devil inside. What could I say?

'You don't have anything bad inside you, little man,' I said, 'You can be good when you want to and never mind anyone telling you about the Devil.' Futile as it was, not saying anything would be worse. I mentioned my exchange to Miss Amponsah over lunch that day, and I asked if he was in care, or abandoned, or something that would explain his self-loathing.

'His mother's a social worker,' she said, as I choked on my school dinner. 'No father. She has four others at home, and the first three we've already had, just like him. Nearly impossible to manage. We do our best,' she said, with a tone that spoke of impotent frustration. I asked her if there wasn't some kind of special school he could go to, or some kind of specialist help he could get. 'He's getting it,' she said, thumbing towards her TA and herself. 'Us. We're the special help he gets. We try to speak to the mother, but she just throws her hands up and says she doesn't know how to control him, and that he's gone to the bad. He's five,' she said, looking almost apologetic for her profession, all children, and the world.

Pupil aspirations

We create ourselves; consciously or unconsciously. If we believe that we're kind, or greedy, or nasty, or stupid, then we often tend to act that way. This is a complex area of contested psychology – are personality traits inherent, predetermined, developed or subject to our freely made choices? – but I can reasonably claim some consensus when I say that our aspirations are enormously important to our self-image, and what we eventually decide to achieve.

How much effort do you think that little man will put into his grades, his behaviour, his future? Not a lot? None? Of course not:

he's a bad seed. Bad seeds don't grow anywhere nice. If a teacher spends all day long telling kids they're horrible and won't amount to anything, some of that mud is going to stick. Forever. This doesn't mean that we have to be relentlessly jolly, and give them lollipops for merely being less awful than the day before, but it does offer us a clue how to inspire and motivate some students.

All our conduct with students needs to be positive. We need to believe in them a bit more than they do. Some of these kids get told – *told* – by their parents that they're no good, or useless, or a waste of space, so we need to tell them that they're not. And I know this is true, simply because they are all human beings, despite what they attempt to persuade you. Even the worst of them are capable of goodness and some measure of greatness.

Be positive; tell them their behaviour disappoints you; tell them that they are capable of better; tell them you care about their education so much that you are prepared to be tough with them in order to achieve success with them. Nothing in this approach prohibits being stern, hard and demanding. I tear my hair out when I hear teachers being advised not to criticize work or bad behaviour. Telling it like it is is a vital step to achieving respect and results. And so is being supportive, stern and helpful. Plus you will earn their respect, which they may never acknowledge until they leave school, but will provide oil for the gears of your classroom.

If you want students to do well, they have to think well of themselves, and they have to believe that you do too, or believe that they can. No student ever busted his ass for a teacher whom they thought despised them. But you can be the only person in the world that believes in them, and that can make all the difference.

Self-esteem

There is an enormous load of guff written about this topic. A recent cultural phenomenon has been the almost universally accepted axiom that we should follow our hearts and just 'be ourselves'. What is this, a Disney movie? Many, many educational practitioners will attempt to sell you the snake-oil of self-esteem. 'The reason pupils misbehave is because of low self-esteem,' they will claim. 'Low grades? Low self-esteem,' I have heard. 'Crappy weather? Low self-esteem.' This just isn't true. Self-esteem is such a nebulous term that it is hard even to agree on a consistent definition. Does it mean strong belief in one's views? Does it mean confidence when speaking? Does it refer to having a plan and sticking to it?

It's a complex concept, and certainly can't be proven to have anything more than an incidental role in behaviour, motivation, kindness and manners. I've seen quiet, shy kids who have unshakeable faith in their moral principles; I've seen loud, arrogant show-offs who crumble in the face of contradiction, or any apparent loss of face or status. High self-esteem can be cockiness; low self esteem can mask carefulness, a desire not to be wrong. So it's not enough just to tell students that they're 'the future' or 'the most important people in the room'. We mustn't fill their heads with well-meaning praise and cuddles, despite their often obvious failure to prove worthy of such laurels. So being positive with them doesn't mean being unconditionally congratulatory; it means saying 'well done' when they deserve it; and 'you need to do better – and you can; here's how' when they don't.

Inclusion

This is one of the great crimes against children pulled off by the state in the last twenty years. Since the late eighties it has been DfE (Department for Education) policy to try to keep children in mainstream education as much as possible. The argument is that children should be habituated into conventional social norms, and if they are removed into a specialist environment they become institutionalized. This argument has a little merit, especially as it was originally aimed at handicapped/disabled children who were shunted off to Blind schools etc, for reasons that had as much to do with society's discomfort as the desire to deliver tailored education. Originally the policy was explicitly not aimed at poorly behaved children.

But that's what it became. The result is that children with extreme-spectrum behavioural problems (or 'very badly behaved kids') spend their whole careers disrupting learning for hundreds of their peers, for years, and making teaching in the UK a famously difficult enterprise. Until this changes it serves no purpose to rail against it too much – accept it as a parameter of the job and make the most of it, otherwise you'll destroy yourself.

Schools need to confront this, especially since recent reforms to exclusion guidelines. Seriously; class sizes, risk assessments, Citizenship, Curriculum – take a ticket and get in line. In March 2009

WAITING FOR QUIET.

the General Teaching Council (phased out in 2011) banned a teacher, Alex Dolan (now a successful broadcaster) from the profession for twelve months. Was she caught stealing or endangering students? No, she had worked with Channel 4 to film a documentary (*Dispatches*) that exposed the depths of behaviour that teachers now routinely face in many classrooms, especially new teachers, or those on supply. Using a hidden camera, she taped horrifying footage of the contemporary legacy of inclusion. The fact that she was punished rather than celebrated tells us a lot about the nature of the modern teaching institution.

Year six the next day felt a bit more like it. They were recognizably above waist height, and wore shirts and ties as if they had put them on themselves, rather than in the tragic, slavish manner of monkeys wearing bow ties dressed as waiters. I met my first male teacher, which reassured me that I wasn't entering some sort of inappropriately dressed harem (although I had once been solemnly advised by a friend in the bar trade that all male primary teachers were gay, like air stewards, because it 'stood to reason,' as he said. I think his argument lacked the certainty of mathematics). Mr Davis was reassuringly bearded and had the air of a slightly strict children's TV presenter: 'Let's have some fun, but let's do it sensibly,' etc.

Having fun

Having a sense of humour is a very useful asset for a teacher; it helps preserve perspective, and therefore your sanity. But the teacher who tries to be an entertainer needs to question why he has chosen teaching and not, for example, being a clown at children's parties. Be funny if you are funny, but even if you are, keep it to a minimum or they'll think you're an idiot. Once you have a good relationship with them you can ease off a bit, but for God's sake don't try to ingratiate yourself to them at the start by making them laugh. You will spend your career in Hell.

Growing up

Little children become big children. Perhaps you noticed? At the reception stage, many of them can't perform basic survival or hygiene tasks without assistance; their emotional reliance on authority figures is enormous, and they can be very distressed by the absence of routine and familiar faces. Their moral sense might be limited too; many of them are unable to perceive right and wrong beyond what promotes or denies their self-interest. Their focus will be short, and their stamina will be variations of low. And, of course their ability to comprehend content will be substantially circumscribed.

The change from pre- to post-adolescence is like falling off a cliff for some pupils; others make the transition more smoothly, or at least in ways that don't impact on your classroom (They may, for instance, write dreadful poetry, but as long as it doesn't stop you teaching about continental plate drift, that's their concern.)

I've just wasted good ink telling you that little kids grow up. So far, so bloody obvious. But one consequence often missed is that we need to be aware of where our kids are at, in order to appreciate how we should handle them, or get the best out of them. Example: when my nieces were two and they wanted to toddle off across the road, or walk towards an open fire, did I negotiate with them? Or discuss the options? Or ask them if they really wanted to do it?

Of course not: they were told 'no,' because we intuitively appreciate that they're not developed enough to make survival–critical decisions for themselves, and that they'll need guidance, and pretty damn firm guidance at that. As they get older, we can discuss the different shades of grey in moral actions, when some things are sometimes right, and perhaps sometimes wrong. Later in life, if they want to they can study philosophy, and end up in catering jobs for a decade. Up to them.

So please don't ignore these truisms and enter into pointless discussions with students about 'why they did that' or 'let's discuss if what you did was wrong.' You need clearly to set an example, set the bar for what is acceptable and what isn't. The answer to 'why did you do that?' is usually 'because I wanted to,' or, 'because she was annoying me,' which isn't very helpful to a discussion. Remember that they are kids – they are learning to be adults, but they're not there yet, and it is your intrinsic duty as an adult and a teacher to help them get there, as we were helped by our seniors. Until Hell freezes over, this is the paradigm we need to work with. The day I ask a Year five pupil what he thinks the class rules should be is the day I ask a High Court Judge whom he fancies to win X-Factor. I rest my case, m'lud.

Lessons with Mr Davis started to resemble the kind of lessons I saw myself teaching in the future. Time was broken up into dedicated segments: an hour for mathematics, an hour for literacy, an hour for drawing their mums. Nothing fancy, but embryonic subjects and lessons. Behaviour was, if not impeccable, at least tangibly the norm, and the lone mentalists who tried to roam the classroom, hungry for mischief, were tracked down and netted like they had a bounty on their heads. I could see in these ones' eyes that they hadn't adjusted to the higher years yet, and they obviously yearned for freedom and fields.[9]

Just before lunch the kids were looking at the story of Easter and working in groups to make a poster, or possibly a draught excluder. Sitting by themselves were two children, a boy and a girl, reading a book. By now I was wary of the various issues that children brought to the classroom, and the teacher was leaving them alone, so I carefully asked them why they weren't joining in.

'We're Jehovah's Witnesses,' said the solemn boy, and his sister nodded agreement. He spoke as if his answer contained every premise needed to finish the syllogism of his argument, but I was still on first principles.

'So why don't you join in?' I said, on the assumption that religious children would be eating religious studies up with a spoon. Foolishly.[10]

---

[9] In some countries, like America and Poland, children are routinely held back a year if they don't appear ready to progress to harder work. There is some merit in this system, although it must be odd to see pupils with acne and moustaches reading *Teletubbies* primers.

[10] Other common rookie mistakes: English kids enjoy English and old people like History.

'Mummy and Daddy don't want us learning about other religions,' said his sister, getting braver. From my (very) limited understanding of the subject, Witnesses were a branch of the Christian Church, and the Easter story wasn't exactly Norse mythology. What a minefield.

Religion and culture

Such a minefield, in fact, I'm surprised Princess Diana didn't stick her nose in. Everyone and their Maiden Auntie has a strong opinion about it, particularly in the school environment. At parents' evenings I tend to get two types of question: *is there too much Christianity taught?* and *Is there too much non-Christianity taught?* The former is usually pitched by middle class agnostic parents who seem to be unaware that we're not allowed to convert them by the sword, like a Jesuit mission in the fourteenth century. The latter usually comes from people with swastikas tattooed to their foreheads, watching the clock in case they miss *What Katie Did Next* on ITV3.

Two reactions to my week in a primary school; first of all I enjoyed myself far, far more than I expected. The children are so friendly, so desperate for your attention, so emotive, that it's impossible for even a paedophobe like me not to warm to them. My second reaction (and the overwhelming one) was Oh God no, please God no, don't let me ever work in Primary School. Sweet Lord, no. You're either a primary teacher or you're not. You either get potato prints and runny noses and crying and tiny people who can't tell the difference between a toilet bowl and their tights, or you don't. I entirely, genetically, culturally, atomically don't. You would have to peel me from the ceiling like Tom the cartoon cat.

My week in Primary School was over. The seal on my teaching coffee jar had been satisfyingly popped by the spoon of experience. I could practically see myself in my own classroom, strolling up and down and addressing my students with indulgent jolliness. Although I didn't realize it at the time, I was precisely one inch closer on a journey to Tibet and back, walking on my hands, with nap breaks. But it had the USP of convincing me until Judgement Day that Primary School was not my bag.

Then came another kick in the pipes: I couldn't even find a secondary school to go to, given that I had as many contacts in secondary education as The Queen does in Eastenders. Luckily the White Knights of the TDA came to my rescue, and with a little pressure, they provided me with a school that was amenable to greenhorns like me gawking and stumbling around their classrooms for a bit.[11] My lucky host was an all-girl comprehensive in leafy West London.

It was a lovely school, although at the time I had no more ability to discern this than a Martian would be able to distinguish between two identical jellyfish. Well, they're all the same, ain't they, these jellyfish?[12]

George Wrigley met me at the entrance to the department, a man of late-middling years who looked exactly like a kindly priest played by an older Gregory Peck, which is what he would later become (not Gregory Peck, as I believe that job was taken, but he did later ordain as an Anglican Priest). He took the time to explain patiently as much about the entire secondary education system as he could in the five minutes between my arrival and his first class, and I started to get the impression that perhaps teachers at the big school worked a little bit differently from the elaborate nursery settings of primary education.

I asked him if there was anything important I needed to know before we began. He thought for less than a second.

'Always make sure you're never alone with a student,' he said seriously. 'And if you are, make sure you keep the door open.'[13]

So we rushed into the first lesson: crumbs fell from my chin in slow motion as I grabbed my briefcase and followed him in, like the trailer for Bad Boys 2, slow motion (without the cars exploding behind us, or sunglasses. And with the addition of elbow patches and M&S ties. It wasn't really like a Jerry Bruckheimer film at all in fact; it just felt like it). I got an attack of nerves like I hadn't felt since a riot broke out during Euro 96 in Soho, and entered my first big classroom.

---

[11] Let me remind you that for the school there is no immediate benefit other than the satisfaction of helping the world. That's as close to pure altruism as an institution can get. Of course there may be significant backhanders going on I don't know about. Anything's possible.

[12] They come here, stealing all our jam jars, 25 million of them in one council house, breeding like invertebrates. I'm not racist, but they're not like us, are they?

[13] This is good advice. We are endlessly vulnerable to accusation, and even the innocent are suspended and cast out until allegations of misconduct are investigated. The damage to your reputation, career and life can be immense, even if you aren't guilty. I'm not sure exactly how a propped door can make the difference, but perhaps it's purely symbolic – for both parties. And for God Sake, don't **lock** the door, which has a symbolism of its own.

Making the most of your secondary school observation

As with the primary observation, the whole point of the process is to provide you with some big, bold brushstrokes of experience that will both test your commitment to the profession and also sharpen up your understanding of what it is you're about to embark on. Some things to look out for:

1. *Behaviour:* This is always my first, second and third priority for anyone new to the profession. You may end up in a school populated by compliant robots; more likely you will have to deal with children who are less than angels and more than devils. So watch carefully how children behave; how they are when they're alone, when they're in groups, and when they're with the teacher. Which teachers do they behave for? Why is that? When do pupils misbehave? What do you think the triggers are? What would you do? Don't worry if you don't have definitive answers for these questions – I don't, and I write a bloody behaviour column for the TES group. Learning to manage behaviour is a process not a destination.

2. *Special Educational Needs/Gifted and Talented Pupils:* try to spot which pupils are at either end of the ability spectrum, and how they are catered for. What effect does it have on how they work and behave?

3. *The Curriculum:* this sound a bit daunting if you're new, but try to find out what exam boards the school works to, and what the content is like. Does the teacher work to a specific plan, or does the department wing it? What do you think of that?

4. *Timetabling:* what is the school day like? How long are lessons and breaks? Does the time of day affect behaviour and learning, and how does it affect the teachers? When do they get breaks, and when are they busiest?

5. *The Staffroom:* what are teachers doing in their down time? Do they get any? Is the mood poisonous or positive? Do staff welcome or exclude you? Why do you think this is?

6. *Duties:* what do staff have to do in addition to their teaching requirements? Do they monitor school areas, or perform any functions in between lessons?

7. *Styles of teaching:* Although the craft of teaching will still seem a bit esoteric to you at the moment, you should also look closely at how teachers operate in the classroom, and try to imagine

which style you would prefer, or which one most closely reflects your own character and aims. Some teachers are matey, some stern, some work through textbooks like they're memorizing the Koran, others freestyle it with discussions and spontaneous exercises. What's your flava?[14]

How is this all to be gathered? Speak to your mentor/liaison to discuss a timetable that covers several subjects, age groups, syllabuses and teaching styles. Ask to shadow them during breaks and duties (but don't crowd the poor beggars; I'm sure you're adorable and they may love having you, but assume they will need some head space from your attentions). And if you're brave, branch out and speak to people in staffrooms, playgrounds and public areas. Try not to walk into anyone's classroom. Or the Head's Office, unless you've decided not to be a teacher anymore.

Twenty five girls were walking in at the same time as I did, which presented me with the Hell of where to sit, which as all British people appreciate is one of the most horrifying social situations to find oneself in. I stood at the edges like an enormous lemon until everyone sat down, which they did with grace.

He handed out sheets and wrote on the board as they settled, and so did I. 'Mr Bennett will be joining us today and for the rest of this week, so I hope you'll make him very welcome.' They looked at me like I had crawled out of a Stranger Danger poster.

'We're doing Noah's Ark,' said George to the class, and proceeded to go through a critical analysis of how believable the Genesis story was, rather than the more plodding Jackanory narrative I remembered from my own childhood. I noticed this with absent approval, because I was more interested in watching the old master George at work. It's a strange feeling, watching an excellent teacher. Because we've all been at school it's like déjà vu, and buried feelings and memories come flooding back. Doubling the peculiarity was the feeling of being a fly on the wall, observing, unseen. It wasn't unenjoyable; slightly voyeuristic but endlessly fascinating, the God's Eye view.

George had other plans.

'Perhaps Mr Bennett would like to take this next segment? We're looking at the construction of the Ark, and I'm sure Mr Bennett knows a great deal about it he could share with us.' He passed a piece of paper to me. And I actually looked around in case there was another Mr Bennett in the classroom to whom I could pass this enormous turd, but there wasn't. He was asking me to 'take' the class.

---

[14] The esteemed educationalist, Craig David.

Take the class. Where?

The paper he gave me was summarized from the Bible, describing the exact dimensions of Noah's Ark, and jolly precise they were too.[15] *I felt a bald, vertiginous horror and froze in panic.*

But ... there was a lot of text. 'Right,' I said in a voice constructed of egg cartons and sellotaped confidence. 'Who can read the first few paragraphs about old Noah then?'[16]

Hands went up by magic, despite my every intuition. It's an odd sensation asking strangers to do something, and seeing them actually doing it. In my previous career, I could get hairy-shouldered Serbians to lift crates up five flights of stairs, but that's because I signed the wage cheques. Plus I had their passports. But to see pupils respond to your request ... I know that this could be misinterpreted, but it's a thrill. I'm sure there are some Cromwellian figures out there who never for one moment doubt that their word is essentially imperative (and I imagine they didn't get told 'no' very often by their mummies), but for me it was brilliant.

I picked a likely lassie, who started reading about the dimensions of escha-tological lifeboats, while I gathered my wits. I had no idea how long I was stranded out there, drowning in front of a room of teenage strangers. The words ran out like grains of sand in a time glass, counting the seconds to my inevitable humiliation, delayed not dispelled. The class filled with silence. And an idea blossomed.

'So, Noah's Ark, eh? What do we think of that then?'

And the hands went up again.

As I walked around I looked at them properly for the first time, as opposed to letting them blur together into a pleated, burgundy-clad, twenty-headed hydra. It was interesting; very multiracial. As I found out later, we had Anglicans, Pentecostalists, two Muslims, a Jew, three Catholics, and ...

I walked up to a table with two young ladies who had customized their uniforms into Halloween costumes[17]*, and customized their faces to look like Marilyn Manson. I thought the school was uncharacteristically liberal to allow them to wear the white death mask of cadavers.*

'So girls, what do you think of Noah's Ark, then?' I asked. They looked uncomfortable.

'Well it's not that we want to be rude to Christians or anything, but we

---

[15] You can check if you like. Genesis 6: 14-16. Bronze Age IKEA instructions.

[16] This is one of the oldest teacher tricks in the book. It is easily the most successful stalling gambit since Sparta jammed the pass at Thermopylae.

[17] I care not a jot how square this makes me sound. It's the privilege of anyone over twenty five to find teenage fashion laughable. I mean – low-rider baggy jeans hanging off someone's backside. I mean, *really*.

... well, we just think it's all made up. There's no way the Ark could have been that size and held so many animals. It's just a myth.'

'Ah,' I said, 'So you're Atheists, then?'

'No sir. We're Wicca.' A beat.

'Really?' I said.

'Really,' they both said, like the Midwich Cuckoos. I felt like telling them to cut it out. I imagined they had listened to too much 'Cure'.[18]

George put me straight later. 'No, they really are Wicca. Their parents are White Witches and Warlocks. Lovely couple.'

I was so far from Kansas, I was in the Urals. I was in Sasnak.

Leaving the school was like saying goodbye to Lassie. I vaguely hoped they would say, 'To Hell with the rules! We likes the looks of ya, sonny. Stay and sail with us!'[19] *George was ordained a year later in St Paul's Cathedral, and I was there to see him take the cassock in a ceremony that Elton John would have appreciated.*

But I didn't have long to wave my hanky and weep. I had chalked up my flight hours. I was in.

Working with your mentor

A word about the people who will be responsible for you during these observation experiences. Schools will assign you someone to look after you during your time in the school; they are there to orient you, take you around the school and give you literature to read, policies, OfSTED reports, etc. This person may or may not also be your academic mentor throughout the experience, and act as your daily contact point. Remember that these people are doing so for many reasons: they may have been told to; they may be keen to encourage others; they may embrace your visit or resent it.

This doesn't mean that you should deserve or expect to get less out of it than you need, but just to help you understand that you should enter into the project with the right amount of humility and gratitude. Schools don't get any extra money for doing this, and teachers don't either. So if you find yourself in a primary or secondary school, be sure to thank everyone, and respect the ground rules they outline for you.

They will also undoubtedly be very busy people; people in schools normally are. In other words, if someone's got a spare moment,

---

[18] Or was it 'The Cure'? Pesky definite article. Batman has the same trouble.

[19] Strangely, this never happened. Perhaps they weren't pirates.

it's worth more than gold or saffron. They won't be able to reflect expansively with you, or take leisurely strolls through discussions about education; they'll as likely be teaching, planning and looking after you, all on the hoof, and all simultaneously with having their lunch and probably phoning a parent too. So if you need something, if there's something you don't understand, if you want to find out about a topic that interests you, take charge of your own training and find a way to find it out.

For instance, write down a list of things you would like to find out about, and then speak to your mentor about who you could speak to. He or she will be grateful that you've taken the time to lead your own learning, and it will allow them to involve others in looking after you. And don't be surprised if they're too busy to engage with you in Socratic ping-pong about the National Curriculum; give them space, and wait for the right moment when you're both at liberty.

Even then, I was still busting my ass managing a restaurant in the West End of London to make ends, if not meet, then at least see each other through binoculars. Saving money is about as natural to me as breathing underwater, and I was managing to put aside about 50p per week, a nest egg I looked forward to busting into when I'd run out of Pot Noodles and handouts from soup kitchens. Working full time, I'd always been able to indulge in luxuries like walls and a ceiling. Now I was going to go from that to essentially pocket money, I did what I always do, and fastidiously ignored my imminent penury. I like to think of it as 'putting on a happy face.' Credit recovery agencies call it 'Christmas.'[20]

---

[20] We communicated so much we were practically dating. Actually, when I say 'communicate', it was actually a bit one sided. They called, I never called back. Perhaps I hurt their feelings. I thought it was better that way. I didn't want to lead them on.

3 | Teachers teaching teachers: *Inside the secret garden of teacher training*

I really should mention at this point that in order to afford to complete my PGCE, I had to make a lot of compromises in my life. Going from a steady income to a bursary-driven life of academic penury nearly gave my bank account a fit, if it had anything left in it to convulse. Never much of a saver (see: witless, profligate, prodigal, knucklehead), I had nothing to rely on apart from bursaries, grants and loans, which came at enormously inconvenient intervals. There was nothing else for it but to tighten my belt past the last eyehole until it went through itself like a Moebius Strip. I also moved into student halls for the year-long duration of my Teacher Training. It felt like twenty.

Finance

If you're completing your ITT as part of an undergraduate degree, or if you are working through a PGCE, you may qualify for funding for your tuition fees (see the link in the Appendix). This is in recognition of the fact that teachers are a key sector of the economy and vital to the continuation of society's intellectual and skill sectors. See? You are special, just like you always suspected.

Student loans

All students are eligible to apply for student loans in order to provide finance for every year in education. These have a variety of ceilings depending on your circumstances and existing finances. Check the TDA website for more details, as these incentives change from year to year.

Earning while learning?

Part-time work is also a possibility; weekend work, or if you are lucky enough to have a pre-existing career you might be able to bring some work home with you, particularly if you are freelance or work in copywriting or IT support.[1] But you will have to face the reality that any teacher training will take the lion's share of your time, and other things will have to be fitted in around it. I managed to keep working on Sundays.[2] Many trainee teachers take part time jobs in a casual capacity that allow them to top up their finances while having a relatively stress-free occupation that they can forget about when they go home. Ignore the burdens of the training year at your peril. It will demand your attention, so give the beast room to breathe. And give yourself a chance to learn.

Employment based training

Employment based training routes will offer their own financial rewards, which for many people is their raison d'être; the starting salary package isn't overwhelming, but you could probably survive on it. I have to emphasize that this route requires a huge level of guts, stamina and the capacity to learn independently, so don't be sucked in just because of the dollar signs. Ask yourself: if this the right route for me? Not, 'Is this the most lucrative route?'

Golden hello

Not, as it might suggest, slang for something you'd have to arrange on the internet, but a financial incentive for teachers to choose key (read: shortage) subjects that need more applicants. Of course, if you were considering those subjects anyway, you're a double winner. At present the Golden Hellos range from £2500 to £5000 depending on the subject: choosing to teach RS will gain you the former; choosing to teach Applied Science wins you the star prize.

---

[1] 'Is it switched on? Have you plugged it in? It must be your hardware.' Show me how to sign up for that job, because I reckon I could do it.

[2] Opening up a large restaurant at 7.30am every Sunday lost its charm after six months, as did working six days a week. I felt like Job.

These Hellos are tax free, and paid as a lump sum once you have graduated from your post-graduate degree and taken a place in a state school.[3]

Tax-free bursaries

The extremely good news is that in addition to the options above, there are still good financial incentives to train as a teacher. If you train as part of a postgraduate degree, you are entitled to a tax-free bursary, again depending on the subject you choose to teach. Once again, these are allocated by an arcane process of supply and demand. Shortage subjects, like physics, chemistry or engineering bag the big bucks; areas with less recruitment pressure take the consolation amounts home. Prospective bursary recipients should apply through their Higher Education Institution (HEI) or school-centred initial teacher training (SCITT) provider.

I busted the lease on my cosy flat, sold off everything that couldn't be binned and moved half a dozen boxes into Commonwealth Hall, a reinforced concrete box in a leafier part of Euston. There's not much to say about staying in student halls that's relevant here, other than the fact that you can get used to pretty much anything if you know you have to, and especially if there's an end to it at some fixed point.

I turned up to the Institute Of Education on the last bright day of autumn and returned to full time education after twelve years thinking I'd never see it again. Who knew? It's a strange thing, being part of such an enormous body again. Hundreds and hundreds of faces, of all ages, milling about looking for the coffee machine and trying not to do anything constructive, everyone with a ring-bound folder under their arm. All ages, mind; baby-faced angels just out of university and chalky harridans making one last career change before the Final Career Change.

It followed a standard format: a few months of lectures, some smaller tutorial groups relevant to our disciplines and subject choices. The rest of the year would be spent on two placements in – Holy Smoke – actual schools,

---

[3] All information correct at time of publication, i.e. 2011. If you're reading this after then, we may be getting paid in dollars for all I know, or our economy may have devolved to crude barter after some apocalyptic event. In which case a Golden Hello is the least of your worries, and I imagine I'm writing advice books on how to avoid being eaten by mutant cannibals. Good luck with the teaching, though.

although the thought was too awful to contemplate. These placements would be interspersed with weekly visits back to the Institute where we would be invited to reflect upon what we learned. As I discovered over the next year, that wasn't much.

Lectures at the Institute were just like I remembered from University: enormous amphitheatres of concertina-hinged seats and a distant stage, a screen and a lonely laptop on a café table. What differed substantially from my previous university experience was the content of the lectures.It felt like somebody was telling me how the parts of a car engine were put together, using the most esoteric and technical of terms, without showing me a picture of an engine, let alone letting me touch one. I found it baffling, and lectures were a chore. Even more so, because attendance was an honour system, and I dragged myself through them with an absence of gusto. Of course, as with any lecture system, there were hits and misses. There's an old truism that says secondary teachers are hired because they can teach, and subject knowledge can come later, but university lecturers are hired for their knowledge, and if they can teach then that's a bonus. Now that might be a bit unfair, but I certainly found the latter to be true. Some lecturers were excellent, or spoke about topics apposite and intuitively useful. I remember the lecture on Behaviour Management was stacked up to the nose-bleeds. People were actually standing at the back and sides, whereas normally any obstacle would have been sufficient to deter the casual attendee. But a forty-minute lecture wasn't much help to soothe our fears.

One of the lecturers was a perfectly lovely old veteran who sounded – and unkind observers might comment, also looked – exactly like Robin Williams in Mrs Doubtfire (in his Scottish alter ego, I might add, not as the loveable, hairy everyman divorcée). Sweet but hardly commanding, her lectures were poorly attended, and she must have thought there were only about fifteen pupils on the course because she commonly spoke to empty rooms. It didn't help that she usually brought us the joys of subjects like 'Definitions of inclusion' and other landmarks in academia.

One day Mrs Doubtfire shuffled out on stage, taking the microphone uncertainly as if it were a Martian flute, and said, 'Well, hello everyone … Mr Riggins is ill today, so the lecture on employment routes will be cancelled. So instead, I'll be discussing with you the various perspectives that make up the Indo-Chinese educational experience.'[4] People started to walk out in their droves. It was awful; they just stood up, thought, 'b*gger it', and left, in plain view of that poor old lady. The final nail was driven

---

[4] I made that up. She might have said she was bringing out pictures of her holiday to Thurso, for all I remember.

home as she watched them leave, with a dismayed look on her face, and said into the microphone, 'Oh no, oh … please don't leave. Please, don't leave.' It was awful.

Back to school

Teacher Training providers come in many shapes and flavours, not unlike dogs. You will of course have taken many factors into consideration before selecting one: you may have looked at reports of their pass rates; their track records as centres of research and other indicators of academic excellence; the recommendation of a friend, a colleague or professional teacher. Or you might have chosen your college because it's on the way to Tesco and won't that be handy? Of course, you may have struggled to find one and ended up going through an elaborate clearing process. Whatever: this book assumes you're in, or will be.

Don't sneer at this: it might be the first indicator you have that you make the grade. It's extremely easy to become disheartened in teaching, particularly in the first crucial years[5], so take this acceptance as a (very) tacit compliment. You can do it. Somebody else certainly thought so.

You will find yourself in a large community of people of all ages, cultures and walks of life. It's an interesting mixture of people, and if you can, I advise you not to burrow off immediately into groups of people of similar age, race, religion and outlook; try to meet as many people as you can and form a broad social network that will both support and revive you throughout your training experience. Most colleges offer a few months of initial lectures and tutorials to familiarize the trainees with basic teaching concepts and ideas to think about, and to start to frame their experiences. Those months will seem like a Shangri-La of ease and indolence by comparison to the rest of your training year, so make the most of them. If there's a lecture: go. If they ask you to read something: do so. I've indicated that some topics will be more useful than others, but what is incontestable is that if you don't read or listen to what you're told, then you'll never know if it was rubbish or vital.

The key thing is to ensure that you attend as much as possible;

---

[5] Which makes you sound like a big baby. You're not. Even if you cry a lot, and wet yourself after staff parties.

with the benefit of hindsight you will be able to assess critically the worth of every part of your course, but you won't have that until afterwards[6] and therefore won't have earned the right to pre-assess.

You will probably be grouped together by subject and assigned a course tutor or tutors. They will be pedagogues from schools, Local Education Authorities or the owlish ranks of academia. They will be, therefore, invaluable guides through your process, so mock them at your peril; they will have been around the block so often they've probably worn a groove in the pavement. But also remember that their opinions and expertise are all part of a greater debate, and that other experts will disagree with them. Take their advice extremely seriously, especially initially, but don't be afraid to challenge them politely to explain their assumptions and axioms. This will be part of your education.

Some subjects will invite their students to complete external tasks, visits, projects and interviews. If this applies to you, then do as you're asked; I was amazed at the number of grown adults who, when asked to travel a few tube stops or do some research on their own initiative, failed to do so. If they apply that attitude to their own education, then it bodes badly for the students in their future charge. If you want to be a teacher, there is a tacit expectation that isn't made clear through your training – you aren't merely expected to be the teacher in a classroom, you will also be the responsible adult in the room.

This puts me in mind of many people who enter parenthood; unless they grew up in a household constantly echoing with the sound of laughing children,[7] even the sturdy, responsible ones are often caught out by how much of an impact a baby makes on their lives, and how suddenly important it is that they take care of the little pink gurgling bundle in the corner. Twenty years later they look at each other and say, 'What just happened?'

Teachers can find this too: if you have left full time employment to study for a PGCE, it can be tremendously disorientating to find yourself free to study, or tied into lectures and tutorials, a strange mixture of freedom and restraint. If you're studying part time, it can seem enormously odd to be a part time carer/worker and a part-time student. If you've progressed straight on to a full-time undergraduate

---

[6] Hence 'hindsight'.

[7] Which I believe was also the name of one of Celine Dion's albums. Or should be.

degree with teaching then at least you have the advantage of being immersed in the world of academia. If you're on a work-based training scheme like the GTP, you won't have time to be stunned. You'll be to busy sailing your sloop through a typhoon of classes and studying to notice.

But the trainees who have spare time and independent learning to do will notice that the opportunities to become a slacker will increase too. If you work hard and take every opportunity, you'll absorb an enormous amount, which you can then assimilate or discard as you wish; but if you slack off, then you'll enter a tough, demanding profession half-prepared, and good luck to you because you'll need it.

What was disquieting was the sense that all this stuff we were being lectured on was important ... but we hadn't a clue how; or how it tied in to the teacher experience. They certainly didn't reassure any of us about becoming a teacher. In fact, one of the principal effects achieved was to remind us of the yawning gulf that existed between what we were, and what we would be expected to achieve. Lectures followed on Bloom's taxonomy; Maslow's levels of human needs; John Dewey and Progressive Education; De Bono's Thinking Hats and Gardner's theory of Multiple Intelligences. It all made little sense. I'm not a complete dullard, despite appearances, and I found it incomprehensible; I think it would be best to say that I couldn't get it in context – we were taught a scoop of psychology here, a dollop of employment law there, a soupçon of behaviour management and a pinch of ICT for flavour. None of it made particular sense and I couldn't quite understand why, apart from a nagging sense that there was something vital missing, something that would tie it together. Of course, there was: it was called experience.

Reading lists

Each TTP will joyfully load you up with reading lists, both suggested and compulsory. The core texts, it should go without saying, need to be tackled first, and in the order suggested by your tutors. Much of the core concepts and terminology used in contemporary teaching will be demystified for you by this process, otherwise you can find yourself sitting in the staffroom or the lecture hall and wondering what everyone is talking about. Although some people object to the essentially bookish nature of research and literature-based enquiry (see? I can talk like an application form too), it's the fastest way to learn the secret handshakes and passwords to the world of education. Again, this is best done reflectively and critically; eventually you will understand what the theorists mean, what the educationalists, the academics and policy makers are talking about, and you will be free to abandon, sneer, adopt or embrace whatever you choose. But first you must read and understand what the current and historical debates are in education.

In fact, many excellent teachers I have met happily admit that such things play no part in their professional lives. But it is far better to be aware of the debates and paradigms that exist in education, even if it only means you discard them. If you fail to learn about the theory behind the practice, you will doom yourself to reinventing wheels that others have already banged together, and to being unable to debate against teaching methods and ideologies that you intuitively disagree with, but you're not sure why.

Be informed. This is the time to get smart about education. Once you start teaching, the opportunities to reflect critically, to research, to ponder and theorize fall off a cliff, never to return. There's little time for navel-gazing once you hit the ground; you'll be too busy planning, teaching, and monitoring to do much by way of self-evaluation, unless your line manager is sympathetic to sabbaticals.

But in the meantime we had bi-weekly conventions of our tutorial group, the small group of PGCE students who would specialize in Religious Studies. My group consisted of twenty-five souls; a Noah's Ark of ages and religions. If we'd stood still long enough, somebody would have given us a grant. Tutorials were led by the grave and precise Leslie, a woman who carried herself with the effortless composure of Julie Andrews and who didn't move a hair without her explicit volition. Literally – we marvelled at her elegant coiffure. Complementing her were Janet and Sue, who sounded like a pair of brightly-coloured children's TV presenters. They were all, I must say, excellent teacher-teachers as far as I could see: positive, confident, and authoritative.

Even then I realized that teaching adults must be a whole different kettle of fish from teaching kids. As the classes progressed, I was appalled to see, for instance, people talking over the tutors as they lectured. This horrified the obsequious teacher-pleaser in me, a tactic that had served me so well in six years of secondary education, and earned me a prize tin of mints in the Year nine Geography competition.[8] And six years of hatred from everyone else, especially if they came to school on the special bus.

---

[8] See? You try to tell kids these days that there's a link between effort and achievement, and they won't believe you.

The sessions were interesting and well planned. We were sent to St Paul's cathedral for a field trip; we were asked to design a student flier for the Neasden Mandir and posters for options evenings (I jumped in boots-first for those kinds of things. There's a frustrated Graphics teacher trapped inside me, having a fag and boring everyone about fonts and CAD (computer-aided design); we considered the role of media and ICT. They were a welcome break from the lectures.

Set tasks

Every placement will set a diet of observations, research projects and tasks to complete as your training progresses. This may take the form of a Personal Development File, a folder of tasks, a placement observation guide, a research thesis or tutor-set tasks. In all cases, try to meet the requirements they set. If on your first placement your program suggests that in week two you observe a maths lesson for behaviour management techniques, then do so; and write about it afterwards. Take notes as you go along, in whatever format you find most helpful. You will rarely have a chance like this again in your career, so make the most of it – the space to breathe, to think, to reflect and amend, although it might not feel like a breathing space. There's no way around it; this is a demanding year, but at least there are pauses built into it where you are required to stop, think and move on.

I say this from experience; I cherry picked my tasks, and put a minimum of effort into studying areas I wasn't passionate about (like SEN education). As a result, I struggled with some areas because I hadn't given the subjects the respect they deserved. It took me years to learn what I should have known in the first place. Use the chance you're given. Which is, after all, what we tell the kids ...

So far, so easy, it was a gentle readmission into academia, and anyway, it wasn't nearly as hard as doing a degree. This was, as I believe it is referred to, setting us up for the sucker punch. Next step was the placement schools. Unsurprisingly, it was felt that a good way of teaching us to be teachers would be actually having us teaching in a safe, supportive environment. The plan was that we would go into schools where we would shadow experienced teachers, watching how the masters did it. Then we would slowly take our first wobbly circuits around the training yard on our tricycles, until the teacher could step back and let us ride the bikes alone, presumably knuckling a proud tear from their eyes as they did so. That was the theory.

If you sense an impending gulf between theory and practice that you could lose a bus in, congratulations: you have more prescience that I did at the time. We were, of course, all petrified to be starting our tours of duty and engaging with Charlie using live ammo. Until this point, children had been abstracts, ethereal algebraic terms discussed in reference to other equally academic concepts like inclusion and multiculturalism.

I, like many, feared the worst. Unfortunately this was an underestimation unrivalled since John Sedgwick said, 'Nonsense, they couldn't hit an elephant at this distan- ...' Right before the Confederate sharpshooters blew his brains out.

Writing essays

You will probably be set a written project. Just like the kids have to do in sixth form, but hopefully better. If you're given a long essay, thesis or research project to do, take advantage of the fact that it will probably be self-led, both in methodology and content. In other words, write something about a topic that interests you. If there aren't any areas of education that interest you, you might think about a career change now. Something about this job has to grab you by the short hairs, or there's no point doing it. Writing an extended essay often terrifies some trainee teachers; it might be the longest piece of writing they have ever done; it might have been years since they have (ever) written an academic essay. Don't panic; there are an enormous number of websites, books and resources to help you pursue a piece of what is usually a scientific enquiry. Your tutor will be the most obvious assistant in this matter, and will be ready to help you through the process. Some simple things to consider are:

1. Have an argument or proposition that you intend to convince the reader is valid. This can be almost anything, but the piece needs to set out to make a claim, otherwise it's just a random collection of unanalysed data. What do you believe about education? Is Gifted and Talented provision a waste of time? Prove it. Do you think the school day is too long? Show them why.
2. Support your argument. Find evidence that supports your view, showing that you have considered a range of sources; literature, interviews, memoirs, statistical data etc.

3. Show you have considered alternative theories, and critically assess their validity
4. Write the bloody thing. It won't write itself. I've tried.

2 | The Main

RULES.

The first placement in particular leaves teachers filled with dread and – unless you've got cojones like a pawnbroker's sign[1] – wracked with nerves about the task ahead. Do not be alarmed. This is perfectly normal.

My first placement school was in south-east London.[2] When my tutors at the Institute discussed it with me, they said it would be a very 'difficult' school to go to, and that many of the kids were 'challenging.' The school had been designated as 'failing' by OfSTED, which normally precluded trainee students being sent there, but it was obvious that we had little option, as placement schools were in short supply, and all Teacher Training Providers had to rely on was the goodwill of the schools to accept trainees. As it turned out, my next school would have had to have been Mallory Towers if the scales were to be balanced.

The train from Euston to London Bridge and then the connection train to the school took around an hour and forty-five minutes in dismal rush hour penury. The early winter weather washed out the world and drained it away into dirty greys. The area, unlovely in the warmest of weathers, was a grim love letter to urban decay in the closing months of the year. There was something in the air: a vague note or two of cold, greasy food; blocked drains and civic ambivalence; most of all, it was hopelessness. I need to point out at this stage that I don't for a second say this with some kind of foppish superiority, or class disdain. Poverty is poverty, whatever colour it comes in. No social class or economic sector holds moral pre-eminence over another; wickedness and vice blossom equally in all soils – they just bear different fruit.

But there is nothing romantic about an area that is poor, institutionalized and desolate, and nothing to be gained from romanticizing it. Eighty per cent of the community were long-term unemployed, and it showed. The only shops open were armoured up to the sills; streets were dominated by monolithic high-rises, and everywhere bus shelters were void of windows, or plastered in graffiti. It was the anti-Hampstead. It would be a long time before Focaccia was available on the High Street. If you wanted Fast Food, gambling or pebble-dashed stonework mottled with damp, however, you were in luck.

I trudged towards it – and trudging was the best word I can use to describe my unenthusiastic gait in such a gloomy Mordor, after an already gloomy and tense morning on public transport. Of course, the train got emptier the closer we got; nobody came here to work. This was where people

---

[1] And therefore, worryingly, three of them.

[2] Long since closed down. The school, not South-East London.

left, sometimes. A rotten high rise towered over everything, and acted as a sentry to the school which was dwarfed behind it.

Behaviour management

Number one fear amongst teachers. Number one. Trainees do not sit at home and nervously swap stories about unsuccessful teaching techniques, about their fears of misinterpreting the Montessori Method, of running out of paper. They worry about behaviour.

Of course they do.

I made every mistake known to mortal man, and more besides. In a way, I'm glad. I think I fell at every hurdle possible at different times. The sliver lining is that it forced me to think about what I was doing, if I didn't want to spend a career in purgatory, and a short career at that. One of the things that stands out most clearly from my work as a behaviour management adviser on the TES website is the fact that behaviour in British schools is far, far worse than you would hope. I get queries from all over the country about handling bad behaviour, and they paint a very broad and worrying portrait of behaviour across the UK. Of course, I'm only getting the behaviour complaints; there are undoubtedly legions of state schools where behaviour is not a significant issue, where children enjoy a decent level of support and discipline from school and home, where education is valued and achievement is celebrated.

But there are an enormous number of schools where behaviour is a significant problem for teachers – and, of course, for the futures of the pupils. Where lessons are routinely disrupted to such an extent that learning is significantly weakened. Where new teachers, especially, will experience baptisms of disrespect and defiance, and pupils who want to succeed will suffer, often in silence, as their education sinks into the floor. There are also many, many schools where behaviour will be inconsistent – good in some areas, poor in others, and the teacher's job is to find out what works and what doesn't.

This experience is particularly exaggerated in the case of new teachers (and supply teachers/cover supervisors), who often get so bullied by their classes that they feel like giving up – and do. There are many reasons for this, some of them political, some of them societal, and I won't bother you with my judgement at this point[3]. But any new teacher will need to know how to tame lions, and they should preferably know a few things before they walk into a classroom.

But only a few things. Behaviour management is an art and a craft: some of it can be taught, and some of it has to be learned on the job. This is unavoidable. Like Buddhist Enlightenment: if I tell you, I'm not really telling you. Teaching at this level operates on an intuitive level, where the teacher reacts subtly and specifically to context and situation, and doesn't simply rely on a set of rigid rules to run his or her classroom. But that kind of skill can't be learned from a book; that kind of teaching is a skill best practised. In fact, it can only be improved by practice: by watching others, by emulating them by reflecting on it and by trying again. It's like a sport, or a skilled manual task. Repetition is a large part of it, but the biggest part of it is doing.

Teaching is a verb, not a guidebook.

Perhaps I've talked you out of reading this part? Not a bit of it. If you're learning to be a teacher, there's a hell of a lot you need to be told in advance, and, more importantly, while you're learning to teach. You can then consider the advice, try it for yourself, and see if you're satisfied with the results. That's the only way really to improve with behaviour management: trial and error. Good advice will help you avoid error as much as possible, but not entirely; it will also help you to see why the good stuff works. These are the nuts and bolts of behaviour management: they are far more prescriptive than the gradual process of learning the art of teaching. They are the opposite of irrefutable, and I offer them up for anyone to challenge. But they work: they work for me, they work for every teacher who has discipline worth a damn, and they should work for you, because they've worked for a very, very long time.

Thwick! A strange noise to my left drew my attention. It just started to dawn on me that there appeared to be an egg on the pavement when the noise went again. Thwick! Thwick![4] Two more appeared as neighbours to the first as I watched. I could hardly believe it. Why on Earth would someone be

---

[3] I'm undoubtedly lying. I won't be able to resist much longer. But this is meant to be advice for training teachers, not Chairman Tom's Little Blue Book, so I'll keep my soapbox under lock and key for a bit.

[4] The official international sound effect for an egg striking a pavement. You're welcome.

throwing eggs at me?[5] *Of course, that part of the official enquiry could wait; I looked up (hoping that the Gods of Irony didn't plant one in my upturned kisser) and saw, high up in a council tower block, a vanishing hood, and the distant chuckle of a child.*

It was, as things went, not bad from the outside. It had clearly had a bit of cash thrown at it, as to one side stood a newish building that could have been a National Lottery Youth Centre, with the instantly unfashionable brushed steel beams of the Blair years, bright painted external panelling, and generous glass walls. Passing that, the entrance spoke more of what was to come; the refurbished glass security box of the entrance; the impressively new-looking reception area, which then branched off into older, less valued corridors.

We were assigned to our Subject Co-Tutors; the people who would show us the ropes and how to tie knots in them. As we were led farther from the more modern entrance, the school tumbled into decay; I could see the decades peel back as we walked. If we kept going I imagined we would see pterodactyls circling overhead, presumably wearing Burberry caps and gold chains. But we stopped short, approximately in the 1960s, and I was introduced to the charmingly mouldy architectural sketch that comprised the Humanities building. It was every shabby modernist cliché of an unimaginative, Stalinist era where, apparently, damp, rust and elegance were unanticipated. My tutor was a plain speaking veteran who was friendly enough, and did his best to make me welcome.

Mentors, tutors and subject co-tutors

If you are studying via a post or undergraduate route, you will have a college/university tutor; when you enter a placement school of any sort you will be assigned a liaison or subject co-tutor, essentially, someone who will take you under their teacher cloak and be the Ben Kenobi to your Luke Skywalker.

These people are key players in your development as a teacher. If they are good at their jobs, take an interest in you, and work hard with you – and make you work hard – then you can have an experience that takes you from rough stone to a polished gem. The converse is true: if they are too busy to look after you properly, don't care enough about you or don't know how to get the best from you, then you can have a dismal time, and learn little. In fact,,

---

[5]   In local logic, the correct question would be 'why *wouldn't* someone throw eggs at me, innit?'

you can even pick up bad habits. So it stands to reason that getting this relationship right can be one of the most important, early-career projects you can work on.

◆ Make sure that you have regular meetings with them. The frequency of these might vary – in a placement school you should be having a scheduled meeting at least once a week. In an academic context, you will meet with your tutor several times a week en masse in the college section of your training, and perhaps once a week during your placements. In addition to that, depending on the provider, you may get discrete, individual time with your college mentor outside these sessions. You should also get a visit in your placement school from your college mentor, who will at some point liaise with your in-school mentor. That's a lot of mentoring. And so it should be: you are in a delicate stage, even if you don't feel it (you probably do). At this stage you need an enormous amount of watching and support.

◆ If you're not getting the meetings, ask for them. If you still don't get them, demand them. Hard, I know, but sometimes you have to step up. This is your future we're talking about.

◆ Ask the mentor to observe you teaching as much as possible. This sounds unpleasant, as most people don't like being observed, but teaching is a doing activity; you only learn by doing it, and it's much easier to reflect on that activity if someone more experienced than you tells you what they think is good about your teaching and what needs to be improved. It's hard to be criticized; but this is the stage where you need it most.

◆ Observe them as much as possible. Again, it can seem onerous, but this is one of the best ways to learn as a teacher. Once you're out of your training year you will hardly ever see another person teach. You may already realize how isolated teachers can be in many ways – just you in a room of twenty five kids; you'll only ever see teachers in the staffroom, dunking their digestives bitterly in cups of tea.

◆ Ask them tough questions: what am I doing wrong? What would you have done? Why am I supposed to teach this/this way?

◆ Write as much down as possible. I know it's tempting to have the meeting and then knock off and get on with something else, but write as much advice down as you can from your mentors in a folder. Then, instead of packing it away forever, take a look at it that night, or the next week; consolidate your learning. If you revisit work periodically, it takes root in your memory. It also gives you the opportunity to reflect on what you've learned, and try to tie it to your experiences since then.

The first day was spent observing – my teaching college had given me a folder with weekly tasks that I had to complete, and day one was unsurprisingly given to orientation. So I oriented. I wandered around the school; I spoke to anyone I came across; of course, I found the staffroom, and was delighted to find that there were two: one smoking, and one non-smoking.

The smoking staffroom was like walking into the TARDIS, setting the dial to 'the olden days', and stepping out. It was an artefact from prehistory, a brown room, painted in mustard and taupe by years of nicotine and smoke. You could have stuck it in a capsule and buried it under the Blue Peter Garden. Everything stank. No stranger to the odd cheeky fag, even I gagged at the prospect of more than five minutes in that – and a laboratory beagle would have said, 'Christ, can't you put that out?' Men in suits that no longer fitted them marked work in books that would reek like a jazz den when the poor kids got them. Teachers sat around listlessly and complained endlessly about minor insults, the inequities of modern education and, inevitably, the children. It was overwhelmingly negative, I have to say. Of course, I had been there for less than a day, and I didn't have any reason to know any better.

Away from my mentor, I felt like someone who had given his North Korean tour guide the slip, and dropped into the backstreets. I asked teachers what the kids were like.

'Horrible,' said one.

'They're not kids,' said another.

'Give up now, while you can,' said a cheery third, who could have auditioned for a part in a fairy tale.

I watched some lessons. Kids shambled in; they had customized their uniforms into more variations than Barbie's wardrobe. We had Angry Street Barbie, Ghetto Barbie, Slutty Teenage Barbie and, of course, Trousers Hanging Round Knees Barbie, who was clearly a role model. They took their seats with disdain, and the teacher got them started. They looked, to me at least, enormous. Their attitude, make up and style marked them out as much older. They were Year nines, maybe fourteen years old. The teacher taught; it was a constant struggle. He had to fight for every second of attention and concentration, batting them back on to the path of education with every heartbeat. I understood the concept of firefighting, such a woeful managerial misnomer; but here it made sense. Whenever he got some kids back working, others at the far end of the room would require guidance again.

And they were children, I understood that. But they looked so frighten-ingly old, like young adults shoehorned into a classroom to learn about something they didn't care about. I watched. I made notes, and I wrote down everything he did to control behaviour, in neat columns like 'low-level disruption' and 'number of warnings given' and 'results from students as a consequence.' I pretended that it meant something to me, but it didn't.

After a few days I couldn't stall any longer; I would have to take a class. But I had until next week to plan it. True to the college's promise, I would only be required to take a reduced timetable – eight lessons a week; rising to twelve as time progressed. It seemed an enormous amount of planning and preparation to me; how on Earth was I supposed to fill just under eight hours of time with rooms full of strangers?

Used, abused or in at the deep end

Wherever you train, you'll be taken from the safety of the college situation and dropped into another world. Treat it like landing on a less fragrant version of Pandora from 'Avatar'. At college you are surrounded by fellow beginning teachers and more or less supportive tutors and lecturers.

An associated danger is that the quality of your mentor or tutor in school will be variable. Schools and departments can accept trainees for a variety of reasons: some of them are noble – they want to pass on their best practice; there's a new Head of Department who's dying to get stuck into some training, etc. Some are less noble – they want 'assistance' in taking lessons, or help designing a new syllabus, or they just fancy a dogsbody.

What do you do if you suspect you're being treated like a gofer rather than an apprentice? First of all, tread lightly; your tutor may not be aware of your feelings. They may think they're doing you a favour by dropping you in at the deep end. That's fine if you're swimming. But if the water starts coming up past your chin then let them know that you're struggling. Few are the tutors who would actively ignore such a discussion. If they do ignore you, for whatever reason, then you need to liaise with your college tutor in order to discuss your next step. What you don't do is just ignore it, and hope it'll go away. It doesn't go away – YOU go away. And you've missed a chance to learn something other than 'I wish I'd spoken up'. This will also help you to avoid the situation where you get your end of placement report and to your surprise they've covered it with dispar-aging remarks about things you weren't aware of yourself.

I suppose the best advice I can give at this point is to remember that the teachers who will be training you at school were probably never themselves trained to teach teachers. When would they have been? They're teachers, just like you will be. They're human, frail and fallible. Don't assume they know it all. In teaching, as in so many fields, sometimes no one knows anything, so help them to help you. You're an adult, remember?

The next week I waited for my first real class to come in. My tutor had looked over what I loosely referred to as my lesson plan, which I had spent all night going over, typing up and resourcing (and believe me, coming up with the goods on a lesson about Hindu Holy Books isn't the easiest thing in the world). Coupled with that was the dread I felt due to my lack of knowledge.

Lesson one was unremarkable. The pupils were for the most part uncomplaining; they grumbled but didn't revolt. Writing happened. For forty-five minutes I held my breath. My tutor sat at the back with his arms crossed for ten minutes before he started marking; he was gone in spirit, but I was glad of his presence. The bell rang.

'Good start,' he commented afterwards. I started to believe it.

First impressions – from the staffroom to the bathroom

People get a hell of a lot of information from you without you even opening your mouth. Sherlock Holmes seemed to do it all the time, estimating what your maiden Auntie had for supper three weeks previously just by noticing the type of clay on your shoe. Most people don't share his supernatural abilities of conjecture,[6] but we do all have a subconscious faculty for reading people on a non-verbal level.

You might think it square, but kids will read smart dress as indicating authority and dignity, and a sloppy, dishevelled appearance as indicating someone that doesn't care very much, or cares more about looking hip than being a teacher. Call it unfair if you want, but these are the associations they make. Assuming you haven't turned up to school in a muumuu[7] or a pair of flippers, what other things should you do to make a good impression?

---

[6] Which he erroneously referred to as deduction, when in actual fact he meant 'induction'. Fortunately, he isn't real, so we can forgive him.

[7] A loose dress of Hawaiian origin, as popularized by enormously fat people, and Homer Simpson.

Day one in the classroom is essential. This is when they will size you up in a second – literally. Most of our impressions about people are generated in the first few seconds of meeting them; everything from their probable social class, income, background, character and so on. These first impressions are incredibly hard to shake, so put effort into making sure the ones you make are the very best you can inspire.

- Be utterly prepared: have all your resources in the room, ready to rock and roll, make sure any worksheets are stacked and good to go, the aims are on the board and your seating plan is written.
- Tidy the room first if you can, indicating that you expect them to come into a clean working environment, and expect them to leave it like that.
- Be on the door to greet them. Be polite, but relatively unresponsive. Meet their gaze every time. If they need to walk around you, let them – don't move. Don't apologize if they have to walk around you, for God's sake. If they cheek you, just stare at them as they walk in, note their faces, and make sure you follow up afterwards.
- Get them to the back of the room, and politely tell them to be

silent. Tell them your name, and your intention to seat them; ignore any tiny misbehaviours at this point – the purpose is to get them into a named plan so that you can start to identify trouble makers. Once they're down, tell them to be silent. Don't ask them, and don't say 'Thank you' if they're still talking. You thank them when they deserve thanks.

Planning lessons

At first the process of planning a lesson seems impossibly arcane and oblique. First of all, don't panic. You don't have to perform the entire time; in fact, it's utterly essential that you aren't the star of the show. Sure, you can talk to them for the entire length of the lesson, but that's a lecture. Lectures are fine in some circumstances (large scale information dumping, especially with older students, but if this is your preferred style, perhaps you should try university lecturing?) but you'll lose your students' attention and they won't learn as much. Why? Because they're not participating. If you clobber them with a teacher-led presentation then they can sit their with their mouths hanging open while you leap and pontificate in front of them. And they can listen. Or they can zone out.

So it's clear that they need to be doing things for most of the lesson, with you merely facilitating their learning, and keeping them on track, probably pushing them onwards as well as keeping behaviour in line. That's the ambition of good teaching, which can be expressed in a thousand different styles.

1. Be aware of the scheme of work/syllabus for that subject and year group.
    If you're lucky, you'll work with a very organized department where the scheme of work has been broken down into week-by-week instalments, with suggested lesson plans and useful resources you can photocopy/download and use for yourself. This level of support is a double-edged sword. It's incredibly useful for a new teacher to have some resources and lessons to use in order to get used to the mechanical process of delivering lessons. But after a while, if the trainee isn't careful, this can become a crutch not a boon, because every teacher needs to go through the process of learning to plan lessons for themselves and experimenting with different styles.

2. Observe other teachers. This is one of the best ways of seeing how other teachers actually teach. By that I mean, what do they actually do for an hour? By this method you'll see the kinds of resources they use, the kinds of tasks they set and the sorts of things they do to keep learning happening. It's good practice to observe as many teachers as possible because no single teacher has the whole story. You can steal as much as you like from other people. Have a look also at teachers in other disciplines and subjects for ideas.

Structuring a lesson

The current educational fashion is to create a lesson with, usually, three parts; a starter, a main body, and a plenary. While there are arguments for and against this approach, it is an extremely useful way to structure your lessons, and once you're used to it, you can then interpret the usefulness of this strategy for yourself. Treat it like a beginner's prop.

The Starter
This part of the lesson serves several functions:

◆ It provides an activity that students know they have to get on with immediately upon entering, preventing them from becoming distracted or having the excuse that there's 'nothing to do'. It means that the majority of your (hopefully charming) students can get on with something.

◆ It provides a link to the previous lesson, acting as a bridge between one lesson and the next, and putting the lesson content in context. Educationalists believe that information and skills are retained far more clearly when they are clearly related to something the student already knows.

◆ It gets their brains into gear, building on and hopefully reinforcing skills you want them to develop.

◆ It provides a lead into the main body of the lesson, perhaps asking them to think about something that will become relevant as the lesson progresses.

◆ It provides them with the aim of the lesson. Most teacher use the starter as an opportunity to let the pupils know what the lesson will be about. This isn't completely essential; you can use it as a 'guess where we're going' activity.

What a busy little bit of the lesson it is, the poor thing. All that in five or ten minutes.

The Main
This part contains the content and exploration of skills you want them to gain in the lesson. Whether it's the Race Riots of the 60s, the reproductive cycle or blocking in basketball, this is the meat. There are infinite ways to deliver this section. There are as many teaching styles as teachers; there are as many ways to teach a lesson as ... well, as you can imagine. Let's do the mathematics: millions and millions, multiplied by the power of imagination ... that's ... that's a very large number of ways to teach a lesson. There is no perfect way in which something can be taught; there are no prescriptions that are correct in all possible universes. Never let anyone tell you their way is definitive. If we are to be true professionals, we need to be able to be creative, imaginative and versatile.

If there is no right way to teach, does that mean we can do anything? That's the wrong question to ask. We should ask ourselves, 'What are the aims of my lesson?' and 'Have they been achieved?' For instance, teaching a lesson on 'The life of Van Gogh', you might have the following aims:

◆ To learn about the events of his professional and personal life, in order.
◆ To understand the relative importance of those events to the painter.
◆ To appreciate the impact he made on Impressionism
◆ To assess his contribution to the art world

We can call these formal lesson aims, which you will probably communicate with the class somehow. Then there are other aims that you might have; hopes and ambitions that you would also like to see, although you might not be so explicit in passing them on:

◆ For everyone to enjoy the lesson
◆ For everyone to understand as much as possible, relative to their ability
◆ For everyone to join in the learning
◆ For pupils to value Van Gogh's life, both in terms of its historical impact and for its own sake
◆ For pupils to become more sympathetic to the plight of the mentally ill

Those are just some of the aims you might have. Then you need to be able to ask, 'Is my lesson designed to do all this?' You can teach any way that is safe in order to achieve these goals. That level of autonomy is exhilarating – indeed, it is one of the best parts of the job – but it can also be terrifying and exhausting because it places an enormous responsibility on your shoulders. That's why you should plan as much as possible in your training period, and execute the lessons. Find out what worked. Copy other people; see if what works for them doesn't work for you. See if you can come up with ideas of your own. There are free websites, like TSL Online that are stuffed with lesson ideas. Believe me, teachers have been doing this stuff for decades; it would be a crime for you not to lean on them a little bit.

Examples of starters in academic subjects:
◆ Copying from the board
◆ Five questions based on previous learning
◆ A 'fill in the blanks' exercise
◆ Listening to a piece of music, with focus questions on the board
◆ Writing down the title, aim and date
◆ Looking at three pictures and coming up with what they have in common
◆ A media clip designed to make them think about their own feelings

Examples of Main Activities
◆ Factsheets and worksheets
◆ Individual work/paired work/group work
◆ Teacher demonstrates a skill, students practise skill, and repeat
◆ Reading out loud from a shared text
◆ Treasure Hunt in room for information
◆ Research on the computer

And so on, ad infinitum. The possibilities are literally endless. There are several pointers that are generally agreed to contribute to good learning activities:

◆ The teacher can lead, but ultimately the pupils must end up doing something. As I say, if you just talk at them the whole time, you might as well be reading them a bedtime story.
◆ Break the lesson up into several activities, or at least give them some change in direction occasionally. Children, especially younger ones, have shorter attention spans, and if you want

them to focus on a topic for any length of time, you need to provide some change, some novelty to keep their interest from flagging.

◆ Give them the opportunity to work with others, as well as working individually. This can mean paired work, small groups, or even the whole class in certain circumstances. This doesn't have to happen every time, but the chance to practise skills with each other, and to share information with others, is useful in developing good thinking. It also encourages collaboration socially. It also encourages them to batter lumps out of each other, steal stuff and cry a lot.[8]

◆ You could have a variety of types of activity. If they start by writing, then perhaps make the next task non-written to provide balance and variety. Then maybe a physical task (even just standing up), and so on.

◆ Keep the pace up. Don't give them one big task for the entire lesson, as this will give the weaker ones a chance to wander off the golden path; if they *are* doing something for the whole lesson, then intervene occasionally to refocus them.

◆ Stick to your timing. You should know roughly when you are moving on from one activity to another. Keep it moving.

◆ Don't be afraid to be flexible. If an activity isn't working, drop it like it's hot. Adapt activities if you think it's going to work better a different way. If you change things, no one will report you to the DfE. Not yet.[9]

◆ None of the above is gospel. Experiment.

The Plenary
This is another important part of your lesson; it involves several processes:

◆ It's a chance to recap over the information/skills of the lesson
◆ It gives the teacher a chance to assess the student's learning
◆ It gives the students a chance to reflect on what they have learned

---

[8] I remember being paired off with the class mentalist when I was a child by some well meaning RS teacher, and being told that we had three weeks to build a Mosque out of Styrofoam and elastic bands. He probably thought he was being a daring experimentalist; after five minutes I was wearing a pile of Styrofoam dust and picking elastic bands out of my eye socket. Cheers, mate.
[9] They're probably looking into it, though.

Amongst other things. This should take the last five or ten minutes of the lesson. Again, there are a million (exactly a million) ways to do this, so the best thing I can do is just suggest a few and let you explore the ways you prefer yourself:

♦ Verbal question and answers
♦ Asking them to demonstrate that they have acquired a skill of some form
♦ Getting the students to do something they could not do at the start of the lesson
♦ Repeat the main points of the lesson in an alternative form
♦ A class discussion on what they have learned implies for some unrelated subject

None of this is prescriptive, nor should it be; good teachers will be assessing student progress throughout the lesson, not just at the end, so in that sense their plenaries can be integrated into the main body. Also, as I suggest above, some starter activities can be used to invoke curiosity rather than just flatly describe the lesson aims. Some teachers start straight into the main body exercises for reasons of time, or because they want to play around with the structure of the traditional three-part lesson. Whatever works is what works.

For formal lesson observations you'll be required by OfSTED to produce a standard three part lesson plan, however, so it is essential that you get used to that structure and become practised in it. First of all, it's a decent enough structure that is serviceable, and before you start monkeying around with form and methodology, you need to get used to the form itself, a bit like a poet having to learn syntax and grammar before he starts mangling it in free verse; otherwise, its just mangling. Walk before you can run. Also, if you don't produce this structure in a lesson plan or an observed lesson, you'll automatically get flunked. So that's another reason.

What else do you need to take into account when you're planning lessons? Oh, not much: just the following:

♦ Can the less able/more able access the lesson, and have I provided appropriate challenges?
♦ Have I identified who they are?
♦ Do I know if any pupils are on the SEN list, and have special educational or behavioural requirements?
♦ How am I using my resources – ICT/physical resources?

- Have I discussed the lesson requirement with my Teaching Assistant, if there is one?
- Where am I going with this lesson? i.e. what is it leading up to? where does it sit in the big picture?
- Where have I come from? Is it building on a previous lesson, or is it more or less stand-alone? And what happens if they don't remember enough from the previous lesson? Do they need to have completed a homework task in order to do this lesson?

Finally: have a Plan B. This will be your parachute if any number of Sod's Law variables drop a load on your head: if the textbooks vanish, if the ICT goes rogue,[10] if half the class vanish on a trip. You can't prepare for every known unknown (or even unknown ones) but you can be ready for emergencies, so have something to fall back on when the sky falls in (and it will, it will).

The second lesson went much the same, although I could see a few of them wriggling more significantly. Some of them did next to no work. A few more lessons went by. My Tutor started 'popping out' of them for five minutes, and as soon as he did so, the kids would look at the door, look at me and then look at each other. I swear I could hear knives and forks being scraped together.

But then he would re-emerge, and the cutlery was put away, and they would scowl and comply; but mutiny was in the air – even I could see it. I wasn't ruling them; they were allowing me to be there.

Then, five days after I began, my tutor left the class and didn't return. Somehow (presumably through a primitive form of childish telepathy) they realized this. And the honeymoon was over. One of them put his pencil down.

'You're not a real teacher are you, Sir?' he said. It wasn't a question.

'I am,' I said. 'I'm your teacher. Get back to work.' I said it, but not only was my heart not in it, it had caught the bus wearing glasses and a false moustache.

'I don't think I'll do any more work today. I'm a bit tired,' he said, looking around the room and grinning at anyone who was watching, which was of course every one of them. Some of them put their pencils down and yawned like they were doing it as a mime. The whole class erupted with yawns.

'Everyone get back to work!' I shouted, louder than I intended. Everyone looked at everyone else with mock surprise.

'Oooooh!' they squealed in different tones. 'Sir's upset! You're not allowed to shout at us, you know.'

---

[10] 'I'm sorry, Dave. I can't let you do that.'

'I'm not shouting!' I shouted.

'It's not our fault you can't teach,' another said. 'Shouting at us isn't very fair.'

'You're not a real teacher,' another said, this one a tall, sly-looking girl who had moved across the room and sat on the lap of the ugliest, most confident boy in the class, the one who had started the revolt.

'You need to get back to the lesson,' I said. 'Get back to your seat.'

'I can't. It's too hard. It's boring,' she said. 'When is the real teacher coming back?' she said, and laughed. Others laughed with her.

There are few things as merciless as being ignored by a room full of people. By this point, no one was working. It's not that they were actively running around treating me like a totem pole – that would come later – most of them were simply chatting to each other with their feet on the desk or their phones out. But whenever I went to any student and challenged them to get back to work, they would turn away like I wasn't there, and reconvene with a nearer colleague. Once or twice I raised my voice to the class, but nothing happened. It was exactly like I wasn't there. When the bell rang five minutes later they left exactly as they pleased, and I felt two waves crashing inside me: relief and impotence, rushing towards each other from opposite directions.

I didn't see my tutor again that day, and as the early winter light faded weakly away, I walked back through the estates and alleys of East Dagenham feeling like the most wretched man in London.

You the man now, dawg

My whole behaviour management approach is neither sexy[11] nor new. There is no way I can dress it up in ribbons and sell it as a 'Behaviour Solution Package' on the internet. I am, so far as I can see, unable to christen it with an attractive neologism and sell pens with my name on it. I am bloody delighted by this fact. Why? Because there has been an extremely odd trend in education (and my soapbox is starting to creak here) that bad behaviour in children is something new, and requires complicated new theories and psychological models to explain and contest; that elaborate tracking and inscrutable paperwork and software will keep children in line; that inspirational speakers and workshops on the emotional needs of children are prerequisites for good classroom control. Good Heavens. I can only assume that prior to these programs, initiatives and

---

[11] It isn't, you filthy pig.

educational demigods, children were tearing each other apart and drowning themselves in the school toilets.

This is a load of guano.[12] Obviously. Good classroom control is free. It won't cost you a penny. You can nick this and tell all your pals if you want, because it's a process that's worked since French Bronze Age hunters herded their children into caves at Lascaux and said, 'Art Class. You paint.'[13] It's based on the most simplistic model of human motivation possible, and it's so easy you could explain it to a child. In fact, spend any time in teaching, and you undoubtedly will.

The official behaviour guru behaviour solution package

Be the Top Dog

Children are curious, adventurous, wilful, smarter and dumber than you'd think. They are also bursting with the desire to do lots of different things as their whims take them. I know this is true, because they're human beings, and that's what we're like. Unfortunately a lot of what they want to do will not be what we want them to do. Case in point: we want them to be at school learning, while lots of them would rather be in the park, or at home dreaming of appearing on Big Brother. This is a conflict of perceived interests. Anyone can see that this is going to cause problems.

Were we in a world where youth automatically deferred to seniority, and authority figures were treated as icons of high status, then this wouldn't be a problem. Whether or not this state of affairs existed in the past or existed at all is completely irrelevant to your classroom. What matters is that they won't automatically do what you say because you're the teacher. So forget about it. Seriously. Don't waste a second thinking, 'But they should be behaving! I've told them to!' That's a valuable second in your life you'll never get back.

You need to show them that you're in charge. At first they might not think that, so your job is to change their minds. Don't ask, 'Why aren't they behaving?'; ask, 'Why should they?' They don't know you. You might be a supply teacher (gone in a day) or a temporary teacher (gone in a week). Which means they think they can get away with misbehaving.

---

[12] Department of Education: official term, number 332/AS5.

[13] Actually, they probably said, 'Uggg ugggggg UGGGGGG!' or something. And then retired to the staff-cave to read the *Jurassic Guardian* and have a fag.

- You're not dealing with rational adults. Many of them will behave selfishly, motivated by whatever gets a laugh, or boredom, or hormones. Rationalizing with classes, while laudable, is mostly pointless.
- They initially value their relations with their peers far more than with you. So they would rather look good to their pals than please you.
- They know you don't know them. Literally; names and faces will be a blur at first. See how long it takes you to realize this: that if you can't put a name to the misbehaviour, you literally can't do anything about it, unless you pin them to the floor with tent pegs.[14]
- They'd mostly rather not be sitting at a desk all day, writing about the Tudors or trigonometry. I don't blame them.
- What they would like to do is sit talking to their pals, planning cruelty upon their arch enemies, and possibly getting a rise out of the new teacher for kicks.

This is not to suggest they are feral, or subhuman. They are profoundly human. They are children, learning to be adults so you need to be that adult. Like it or not, you will have to be the biggest dog in the room. If you have a problem with that, you'll have a problem in teaching. They don't need another pal; they need you to be an adult, to set boundaries for them, and to provide order and structure in their education. If you do this, you all have a chance. If you do not, then you'll be firefighting your entire career, their education will suffer, and you'll crumple with stress. I advise you to take the High Road.

Setting boundaries
- If the class isn't behaving the way you want, then you're going to have to bring the rule of law into the room; your law.
- There will probably be a whole school policy on behaviour, outlining punishments you can use, and when you can use them. There should also be a reward system. The students will be familiar with both, so if you use them, then you show that you are an extension of the whole school teaching team, and not some pathetic loner student teacher that they can kick about like a tin can.
- Familiarize yourself with the names of senior teachers in the

---

[14] Frowned upon.

school responsible for behaviour and general ass-kicking. This might include Heads of Year, Form Tutors, Senior Staff. Don't invoke their names willy-nilly, or they'll realize they should be scared of them and not you, but drop them in from time-to-time to show you know who carries the naughty stick at school.

◆ Tell them what you expect of them, both in behaviour and work; you can do this by a short speech, a handout, anything that shows them you have rules and you expect them to obey. Even if they disrespect this process, you have made a point.

◆ If anyone breaks the rules, take their name, give them a warning or a punishment like a detention if it's serious enough, and inform them of your decision. Do not engage them in conversation on this point. I repeat; do not. The lesson will be ruined by arguments, and it's demeaning for you to argue with students. Let them huff and puff

◆ If you set a detention, then DO IT. Be there, for God's sake.

Class rules
Keep them short, simple and fairly general, while allowing yourself scope to expand. If they're too vague, then they're meaningless, i.e. 'Everyone must respect everyone.' That stinks like a rat in a drainpipe. Avoid being too specific either, or they will mercilessly throw your own rules at you, i.e. 'No chewing gum' suggests that they might be allowed to chew tobacco, or bones or something. I go with the following class rules:

◆ Don't talk over me
◆ Put your hand up to talk
◆ Wait for me to allow you to talk
◆ Treat everyone with manners.
◆ Be on time
◆ Bring equipment
◆ Do all work

That last one is useful because telling people to 'respect' everyone else is like telling someone to 'reach for their dreams' – its meaningless, and also probably impossible. But everyone knows what manners are. You can add a few more rules, but keep it short and sweet. I tend to have one main rule: 'I'm in charge.' It has a ring to it. These rules are hardly groundbreaking, but make them explicit. Then you can't be accused of being too vague.

So far, so uncontroversial. It all sounds so simple, doesn't it? Of course, it's not. Here are some of the things that will upset this process:

1. Pupils will fail to turn up to detention
   Then you need to follow up: this is when it starts getting tiresome. Call home and tell the parents what happened. Be direct, but supportive. Say you need their help for their child to learn. Don't say their offspring are Satanic, even if they are.

2. Pupils will argue relentlessly with you
   One more time: do not engage; repeat, do not engage. You look weak, and reduce yourself to their level if you argue with them. If they won't settle down, then have them removed from the lesson or send them out to calm down. There is nothing more important than the education of the pupils in the classroom. Anyone who upsets that can spend some time in the cooler.

3. There will be so many students misbehaving, it will be hard to know what to do
   Keep taking names, no matter how long it takes, so that you can follow up later. Or at the end of the lesson only let go the ones who definitely behaved. Avoid whole class detentions if it's at all humanly possible, and even when it's not. It's a cowardly, counterproductive technique that will have them hating you, and devising new ways to send you to perdition.

4. You feel like giving up – and do. Soon, you start ignoring blatant misbehaviour in order to have a quiet life.
   Never give up, even when you really feel like it. Trust me. I'll discuss this in more detail later.

Follow Up

This is, perhaps the secret ingredient of behaviour management; this is the Colonel's secret recipe; Coca-Cola's mystery ingredient; this is the thing I should sell on the Internet – the real reason why so much behaviour management goes astray. This is the final part of the jigsaw.

An enormous number of new teachers say, 'I've tried all the behaviour tips – I've set detentions, I've done the whole nine yards … but they're still misbehaving. Boo hoo.' I don't blame them; they get told all of these simple rules and standards to follow, and then nothing really happens. The naughty kid eventually attends a detention or hands the homework in. The parents have been in for a meeting. You have issued detentions to the students consistently for a fortnight. But nothing. They still misbehave. Sometimes it's the same kids; sometimes it's others, but it becomes repetitive and never-ending. Why isn't it working?

Because it takes time. Never give up. This is the element every new teacher needs to understand. This is the Kryptonite. Teachers have two superpowers that the children don't have: we are organized (or we should be), and we have stamina. The kids aren't organized. If they were, we'd be up against the wall before you could say Viva Zapata! They work alone, or in pairs, or in miserably small groups. We are a mighty monolith, the school, the government. We can go all the way; we have the ability to issue sanctions, over and over again. So use this power.[15] If people don't turn up to your detentions, record it and discuss it with the Head of Department, or your mentor, or whomever is responsible for keeping order in that area. Follow up with these people; ask what is being done, and is there anything you can do to help. You are part of a team, which implies two things: they have to help you, and you have to help them.

The second power is stamina or perhaps just patience. Keep doing it. Don't give up. Given a pupil three detentions, three weeks in a row? Do it again. Almost every single pupil will eventually give up, in the face of constant punishment. Of course they will – they're kids, not master criminals.[16] They will usually do anything to escape privation, which for many of them would be defined as not being allowed to play Call of Duty 24 whenever they felt like it. If you keep it up, they almost all crumble and comply. The ones that don't (a tiny minority) will have to be dealt with by extraordinary measures (or, as I like to call it, excluding them), and you'll have to enlist your superiors for assistance.

How long will it take?

Those last few paragraphs are probably the most important advice I can give to a trainee teacher. Seriously. Persevere and things will settle down. Setting a timescale on it is impossible, because it depends on so many factors: the general compliance levels of the pupils in the school, the percentage of Special Behavioural Needs children in the room, your own personal presence, your body language and a thousand other factors. At the risk of setting an impossibly vague timescale: most teachers experience an improvement in behaviour levels after a term; after a full year teaching in school, there is usually

---

[15] It wouldn't be your first choice of superpower, I grant you.
[16] Not yet, anyway.

a marked improvement. By the second year, relations should be on another level, and the teacher should be able to push them harder and expect even more from their behaviour and work – IF they have been applying the rules consistently and fairly.

Don't ...
- Be tough one day and tender the next. Consistency is massively important
- Be nasty. If you EVER say to the class that they are 'horrible' or 'evil' or – God forgive me – you 'hate them', then you will deservedly be poked with a dozen pointy sticks forever, in Hell
- Blow your stack at them. Shouting will get their attention, maybe even cow them slightly for a minute, but actually, after five minutes they realize, 'Is that all she's got?' and your fury will be revealed as empty, hollow and meaningless. Besides, some of them will find it entertaining. But most importantly, it's undignified and makes you look like an emotional fool. What would Sean Connery do – apart from shoot them? Imagine someone you respect as an authority figure. How would they conduct themselves?
- 'Forget' to turn up for a detention/meeting/chat if you are meant to be there. They will realize a terrible thing; that sometimes

they can get away with misbehaviour. That's as bad as never punishing them. Inconsistency will bite you on the ass.[17]

◆ Turn a blind eye to something you normally punish. Just because you're having a great/tiring/hung over day doesn't mean YOUR behaviour should be any different from normal. See above re: inconsistency.

◆ Let them off with misbehaviour because you can't be bothered to follow up. Do your job.

◆ Completely forgive their crimes because 'they were good afterwards'. That means they can misbehave, then get away with it if they act nicely afterwards. Which means they'll never be good *all* lesson. Of course, you can still reduce their detention/prison sentence if they act really well, but never entirely rescind the punishment. There has to be some justice. You are the Law.

Some of you will have noticed a pachyderm in the premises: I said that this will take time. Some of you might have noticed that the timescales I mentioned might even fail to fall within the time you will have within your placement and therefore you may not experience what you might call satisfactory behaviour before your placement ends. This, I'm afraid, is just something that some trainee teachers will have to bite on. You may not indeed. But it's still important that you follow these guidelines because it's good training for being the kind of teacher who does get results in a permanent post; the kids still need to see you trying, or they'll be all over you like tiny, beardless pirates; and because in many cases, you WILL see a distinct improvement before you go.

In one lesson, pupils started running around the classroom (I'm not making that up), up and down over desks, making red Indian noises. I was smart enough not to stand in the middle of it, but what could I do? What options do you have when you've shouted 'Stop!'? Shout 'Stop' again? This was a world where not only was authority not deferred to, it was openly mocked. I had never worked in a situation like it. Inside I could feel myself crumbling; there's only so much humiliation a body can take before it starts to seep in, rusting your reserves of self confidence. Like a flower cracking a paving slab through persistence, they started to wear me down; not dramatically, which would have been easier to handle and notice, but by degrees, layer by layer. Every day I felt heavier and heavier, and every night I slept

---

[17] Perhaps that's your thing.

less and less, while at the same time I started staying up later and later planning lessons.

By early December I was coming home after my long journey in the dark to my empty room – I had that much at least – and staying up till midnight, working and not working, planning lessons with little to show at the end of it. I was chasing my tail and trying to ignore the growing hole I felt inside me, the dark spot that was becoming a pit. I could feel it. I ignored it. The days continued, and so did I, because I didn't know what else to do.

It wasn't that my tutor was careless or unkind: certainly we had discussed the problems I was having, and he had taken great care to give me advice about how to hold their focus. But nothing I did seemed to work, and almost every lesson I was completely by myself.

I taught most year groups, from seven to eleven (or approximately from the ages of 12 to 16), but they started to merge. Some of course were more compliant than others – the younger ones, naturally seemed less feral. Even in the worst classes, it was only really a core of nutters who would seriously disrupt the lesson – but that was enough. Thomas Hobbes said if there 'is one Thief in a City, all men have reason to shut their doors and lock their chests,' and he was right. Just a few, that's all it took, for my carefully planned lessons to fall apart, stitch by stitch, block by block, until it was as if they never existed. Worse: as the most belligerent pupils started acting up, the next tier of pupils decided they would too, or at least give up working, until eventually the outermost ring of pupils – nominally the 'good' kids – would decide that if everyone else was having fun, then Hell, why shouldn't they?

Usually the worst classes were in Year nine; I had been told to prepare for this by good old George Wrigley. They were the perfect storm of hormones, youthful childishness and adult desires and restlessness. They were gangly, unused to the faculties their bodies provided for them, and certain of only one thing: my lessons were sh**. I was beginning to agree with them, frankly.

School Systems and sanctions

If children are routinely misbehaving in your lessons then you should never feel that you are the only rubbish teacher in the world – of course you're not – there's loads of us![18] So don't sit in your classroom, feeling the throbbing vein on your forehead pulse in and out like the Channel tide. Get help from the people around you, because believe me, you're not the only person going through this. My mistake (one of them at least) was to suffer in silence, blame

---

[18] ☺

myself for everything, and try to control a class using the power of my mind. Unsurprisingly, it didn't work.

The whole school behaviour policy

Every school should have one of these: a document describing what set procedures they follow in order to maintain good order. This will describe the types of sanctions you can issue, what kinds of behaviours will trigger these sanctions, and what to do to prevent escalating misbehaviour.

a) You might send the pupil outside for a few minutes to cool off, and reconsider their ways. This should be a maximum of five or ten minutes. The aim should be to bring the kid back in, aware that he was close to seriously crossing a line. This is a good tactic with children who have 'anger management issues', which is another way of saying 'gets angry very easily.' I leave it to you to decide if this is a syndrome or just a description of how they behave.[19]

b) A verbal warning. Many schools use something called a Consequence Code, which is just a system of warnings that indicate first the threat, then the enacting of a sanction. So if a child is talking over you, you can say, 'Billie – C1!' in an imperious tone, and they know if they cross the line again they'll be painting fences in the cooler.[20]

c) A stern look, with strong eye contact and a face full of disapproval. Once you get this right, you'll be doing it all the time. It's like the Jedi Mind Trick.[21]

d) Setting a detention. Spend any time in teaching and you'll get used to this. A short spell with you after school, in lunch time, in break. Make sure that whatever they do in detention (lines, work, an apology) is unpleasant enough to make them mind being there. If you just let them read their book or text their chums, then they won't see detention as unpleasant enough to want to avoid.

e) Talking to them after the lesson. Do this alone, with none of

---

[19] But just in case you'd like me to help: it's a description. If we label and medicalize every human trait, then pretty soon we describe pickpockets as 'allergic to the concept of property' and boring people as 'interest averse'.

[20] I understand that punishing children by telling them to paint walls or build something interesting is no longer encouraged, which is sad if you grew up reading Tom Sawyer. Or Genesis.

[21] These aren't the grades you're looking for ...

their peers to witness it and you'll get the real pupil, not the face they present to the world. This means that you won't have to battle against their prickly sense of embarrassment and peer approval. Tell them what they did was wrong, and why they can't continue the behaviour. I also make sure I tell them that I care about their education, and by default them; so much in fact that I won't put up with their non-learning antics. It pays to be polite, and perhaps a little conciliatory. But make no mistake; this is your opportunity to tell them what the rules are, so don't try to become their pal. They will detest you for it. Show them some steel; show them that you want them to do better and that you believe they can. The two attitudes together are incredibly powerful.

The parents
Often the most forgotten part of the behaviour process. Get the parents on side, and all of a sudden you've got the strength of ten and a naughty stick that extends all the way into their bedrooms. A simple phone call home with an assertive but friendly explanation of why you need their help, can work wonders.

The pupil
Behaviour management is often a process of building up relationships between you and the pupil; at a minimum it needs to be the kind of relationship where the pupil sees you as an authority figure, and one he can trust to guide and lead him. With subtlety and sensitivity the pupils can gradually develop high expectations of you, and you of them, and you can drive them to greater heights. But stick with the coercive relationship, at least at first. If you start off getting them to call you 'Tony' then they will mug you off until Hell freezes over. And then they'll mug you off on the ice.[22]

---

[22] Impossibly, I have George Bush (or one of his more literate speech writing monkeys) to thank for that beautiful bit of wit.

5 | Not waving, but drowning: *Going under on the first placement*

One day I was teaching one of my less objectionable classes when a young boy wearing the full uniform of the teenage gentleman of leisure – hood, baggy jeans so far off his arse they looked like an enormous blue nappy, Burberry Cap – who was wandering around the school,[1] decided to have some sport with me. His cunning game played like this: he would open my door and shout 'W**ker!' as loudly as he could, and then he would shut the door with a slam. Then I would come to the door as the class fell about laughing, whereupon he would scamper off into the sunset. As soon as I returned to the front of the class, he would repeat the process, and so would I. Forty minutes of that.

Inclusion – part two

You will hear an enormous amount about this when you teach. Inclusion essentially means trying to make sure that every child attending school is included in the school community, where everyone feels valued, as a foundation for high quality teaching and learning. This is an extremely valuable goal, of course, and as a teacher you will be expected to try to make sure that no child is left behind in your classroom. In practice this means making sure that you have differentiated your work to a suitable degree that everyone can feel challenged and stimulated: that the work set is appropriate and interesting; that feedback is regular and constructive.

It also means that all groups need to be able to participate in your lessons; these groups are not only on an ability spectrum. Inclusion refers to different cultural and linguistic groups, both genders, those

---

[1] On his way to the library to settle some nagging question about the authenticity of Geoffrey of Monmouth's *History of the Kings of Britain*, I like to think.

with disabilities and the able bodied, those with typical behavioural skills and those with atypical skills.

There is a significant issue within this policy, however, which I have touched upon in my hilarious anecdotes; it also applies to pupils with behavioural issues. Some would call them badly behaved, but I wouldn't dream of referring to them in such an unsympathetic way. Twenty years ago, if a pupil was regularly disrupting lessons, *and* was unresponsive to successive attempts to rehabilitate his behaviour, then eventually he would probably see the backside of the school gates (or 'be expelled' as it was called. They changed it to 'excluded' in order not to upset people who had been 'chucked out of school'. Perhaps they think they won't notice.). The naughty boy or girl would probably get a couple of chances in other schools that would reluctantly take them in, but if they still behaved badly in the last chance saloon, then they would find themselves warming the inside of a Special School, where all the naughty boys and girls went. They weren't very pleasant places, but they were offered tough education – whether they wanted it or not – and the mainstream schools were free from repetitive head bangers.

Now things are very different. Many schools are still unfairly penalized for high exclusion rates, and if they look like they're a bit trigger-happy getting rid of their charges they get told off by the Local Education Authority. It also looks extremely bad for them to show a high exclusion rate, because they imagine that it indicates the school is badly behaved. The solution? Keep' em in; that way it looks like the school is populated by the Von Trapp family. Besides, almost all the special schools in the secondary sector have been steadily closed down since the eighties, so there is literally nowhere for them to go. If they do get excluded permanently from school (and you *do not* want to see the hurdles of paperwork that have to predate that event) then they get sent to the next school which, if it has any space, has to take them in, like extremely unwelcome hotel guests. The school braces itself and thinks, 'Here we go again …'

It's not a satisfactory system. It emerged from extremely laudable ambitions, to rehabilitate society's peripheries within the mainstream community, and to avoid simply turning these kids into another unwanted caste, flushed out of schools, into the special schools, and then on to a life of crime and prison. An enormous amount of research showed that pupils excluded from schools ended up before magistrates within a few years. Other data clearly showed a link between low levels of education and high crime rates, antisocial behaviour, stagnant economic workforces and so on and so on. So the idea of trying to keep children at risk from falling through the gaps in society's safety net is both ambitious and noble. Unfortunately, it has been a disaster.

I've already alluded to the effect it has had on schools: leaders and governors reluctant or refusing to exclude or uphold exclusions on appeal, because it was deemed to make the school look bad, or worse, or perhaps more charitably because they felt that the students stood a better chance within the mainstream population. And perhaps some of them would. But the other side to this enormous coin is the effect that retaining these children has had on the education of the 99 per cent of children who were never at risk of exclusion. I was a teacher for about five minutes before I realized that there was a core of one or two pupils in every lesson who were responsible for making classes extremely hard to teach. And I mean in almost every lesson; the naughty kid; the head banger; the misunderstood; the victim; call him or her what you will. And those children don't just make classes hard to run, they make them nightmarish.

Anyone who has tried to teach a class will know that it takes enormous effort to maintain order or to create it, and an almost trivially small amount of effort to destroy it; it is a truism of life. One determined, unhappy child can make fifty minutes seem like a fortnight if they are wilful, mischievous or persistent enough. Witness my own battles early on in my career and the effect is clear. And as I know from working on my behaviour forum, this is not an uncommon phenomenon.

This is one of the most enormous issues in education, and I'm going to repeat it forever, because although in 2010 it was made easier for Heads to permanently exclude, schools are encouraged not to do so, by a variety of financial and political means. Because good behaviour management can be achieved, and I believe that the vast majority of teachers can achieve it if they follow my fairly simple guidelines, outlined above. But they take a while, and they take a lot of energy, which strikes me as somewhat of a shame, because that energy could be used more profitably instead in planning interesting and exciting lessons, full of awe and wonder, not wasted in planning campaigns to control and neutralize the naughty kids.

Naughty children have been with us forever, and always will be; it's in their job description, and God bless them for that. What I'm referring to are children who, in my opinion, aren't detritus or social waste, but very damaged children – never forget that they are children – whose already blighted lives are not being improved by enforced inclusion. They need to be taught in secure, one-to-one environments by specialist teachers who have the skills to deal with the complex matrices of social, biological and psychological problems that these children face. A teacher in a mainstream class can only deal with the after-effects, the symptoms as it were, of the problems these children face. And dealing with them while simultaneously trying to teach 24 other people means that an enormous amount of lesson time gets flushed down the pan while little Sammy has a screaming fit with the teacher, and the kids roll their eyes and think, 'This is boring'.

Another effect is that once these children are included perpetually in lessons, other children begin to see their behaviour and emulate it; they realize that the boundaries aren't as tight as they once thought. If little Sammy can huff and puff, and he barely gets a detention, then why shouldn't they? Children learn by emulation. If one of the kids gets away with acting out, then others less challenging will copy the behaviour. And the behaviour in school deteriorates. This is a picture that hundreds of thousands of teachers will testify to, but very few people above the level of teaching staff will admit; there is an ocean of disagreement between the policy makers and the practitioners.

And who can blame them? Most of the policy makers have never experienced state school education (and I apply that to both sides of the House, incidentally; this isn't a party political broadcast) and will never know how damaging it can be to retain pupils in schools who should have been out long ago, because they don't send their children there and never will.

I don't want this to sound like the preaching of John the Baptist, but its something that every new teacher needs to hear. You may be fortunate and walk into a well-run school, of which there are a multitude, believe me. But chances are, many of you will work in a school where at least some of the pupils will display off-the-spectrum behaviour, and you need to be ready to handle it. Follow all the rules, above, and dig your heels in. It's a battle sometimes. But once you know that, you can get ready for it.

One day, mid-lesson, when I actually nearly had a class working as a group, a young man burst the door open like Mossad. He wasn't wearing a uniform, and jewellery hung off him like someone had covered him in glue and kicked him through an Argos catalogue. His hair was braided into neat corn rows, and even from the front I could smell him.

'You a supply?' he said, as though I wasn't meant to be there.

He walked in and sat down. Without looking at me he said, 'I'm Danny Webster. This is my class.' I looked at my register. Danny was one of the never-shows.

'You're late,' I said, redundantly, as everything I did was.

'So what?' he replied. I had no answer. What did you do if someone was late? Send them out? They just got there. Surely the object was to get them into lessons to learn, not punish them by chucking them out when they do come in? I caved in to expediency. 'There's a worksheet,' I said, passing him a paper on Hindu beliefs about Ahimsa.[2]

Then I smelled it. The unmistakeable, powerful odour of skunk, hot-housed weed.[3] But my mind wouldn't accept what my nose was telling it; it was preposterous even to imagine. In a schoolroom? I turned round and looked at the class with a sceptical look on my face. They knew I knew something, and everyone stopped to look at me.

'There's a strange smell in the room,' I said deliberately, eyeballing everyone.

'No there ain't,' said Danny. 'Can anyone smell anything?' he said to the room. Everyone agreed tacitly. I went back to work. But the smell was still there, and getting stronger. There was no way I could continue, obviously.

'I can smell drugs in this room.'

I wasn't looking at Danny when I said it, but nobody was fooling anybody. It was obvious where the smell was coming from, and it was obvious who I was talking about. The moment I caught his eye he kicked off.

'F**k you looking at me for? What the f**k you saying man? You saying I got s**t on me? S**t, I ain't gotta take this sh**, you wanna say that to my face? You got the balls to say that?'[4] He was tensed, sitting up in a half crouch.

'Did I say you had it?' I said, realizing that this was going to go one of several ways in the next few seconds. My face tried to say 'placatory' and 'assertive' at the same time. 'I don't know who has it. I just know it has to go right now.'

'Or what?' he said, and he made a good point. Or what? What could I do? In the club I could have snapped my fingers and Danny would have been thrown out like a drunk in a Wild West saloon. Here it was just him, me and any wits I had. The next thing I said would determine if he would

---

[2] Posterity forgot to record if this thrilled him or not.

[3] Which I have to say, does actually smell *exactly* like a skunk's infamous anal defence system, as I can personally testify after a few rambles in Canadian woods.

[4] Isn't it odd how kids from South-East London can talk like they're auditioning for 'The Wire'? I wonder where they get it from? Ah, rap music.

throw his chair away, bounce up to me face-to-face and start swinging his fists. I had seen this hundreds of times before; he wasn't kidding. He had been – or imagined he'd been – slighted, and in front of his peers too, who were obviously terrified of him. Without meaning to, we had crossed over from the playground to the street in a heartbeat, and I hadn't even seen the join.

The bell rang. He deflated, and pulled back.

'Yeah,' he said, 'F**ker,' and walked away into the corridor, where he hugged another pupil like a long-lost brother and bounced off arm-in-arm. The rest of the class left.

I breathed again.

Drugs

A horrible topic to have to mention in a book for teachers, but it's one of those things that crops up all too regularly. Your job, as you might have guessed by now, isn't all about teaching; it's also about keeping them safe among other things, and sometimes you have to keep them safe from themselves and each other.

Controlled drugs are, of course, illegal everywhere; and most schools have an explicit policy banning their presence in the school environment and providing guidance on the consequences of their discovery. But it doesn't need a policy for you to know that they are obviously banned in schools, and particularly unwelcome given the effect they can have on growing children.

Teachers and staff actually have quite a few powers in this area. Head Teachers have the power to approve (with reasonable grounds) searches of a pupil's bag or locker without their consent if there is suspicion of the presence of knives, alcohol, pornography, tobacco, electronic devices and, most importantly here, drugs. In fact, they can even search for and seize legal drugs such as methadone or glue. In the situation I found myself in, I should have summoned a senior member of staff, informed him of the suspicion of drugs, and immediately obtained authorization to demand the pupil open his bag. If this had been prioritized then it could have been done in minutes. If you have a suspicion that pupils are harbouring such things, then get on it like it's a house on fire. This is one of those emergencies you hear about. Keeping drugs out of schools is just about one of the most important things you can do for your pupils that day, that week.

On a final note, I know that attitudes to drug use, especially the less 'hard' drugs, can vary among teachers; some pupils I have spoken to come from Rastafarian families, where cannabis use, for example, is seen as having a religious context. Whatever your personal views, your legal responsibility is clear; these drugs are illegal, and there is no way on God's earth that children should be exposed to them. They need every brain cell they can get, and if you find yourself advocating them in any way, you do too.

I had to learn about marking. It said so on my schedule, so I approached my tutor who sent me to a visiting expert to ask for some guidelines. We sat down with a pile of GCSE classroom tests.

'Read that,' she said. 'What mark would you give it?' I looked at the student scrawl in front of me. It said something like, 'Muslims shood be against abortion because there God is Ella they where turbans.'

'What's it out of?' I asked. I had no idea what to do. 'I have no idea what to do,' I confirmed.

'It's out of four. So what do you think that would get out of four?' I read it again. It was badly spelled, didn't really answer the question, and only contained tangential references to anything like an answer. 'Nothing?' I hesitantly offered.

'Nothing? No. Look – he mentioned Allah.'

'But that's not really answering the question,' I said, confused.

'Look,' she said, sounding cross, 'Are you questioning me on this? I know the chief examiner. That gets one mark.'

'OK,' I said, confused, 'It just didn't seem relevant.'

'It is. Just accept it.' I could tell I had annoyed her and I really didn't know why. 'Work through the rest of these papers – those questions are out of two, those out of six, those out of eight, and those out of four. Get as many done as you can and I'll be back at lunch time.' And with that she left. I picked up the first paper and wondered whether what I was looking at was good, very good or terrible. My training in marking was over. I got on with it.

Marking, monitoring

You will be expected to know three things in particular about your pupils, not unreasonably:

1. how well they are doing
2. what they are capable of
3. how they can improve

None of these is as simple as it might at first sound. At first, the problems aren't obvious. Surely it's easy to gauge all three of these things? Example: you've just taught the class a unit on the Tudor Kings. At the end, you set them a test; it's composed of twenty simple factual questions about who was King, when, and which Queen he was divorcing at which point. Mark the answers, right or wrong, out of twenty, and you have a clear score. Easy. Now you know who is smarter than whom. Report card sorted, and everyone's happy.

It gets better. You can set them the same test in a week's time mark it again. Voilà! You've seen how much progress (or not) has been made. You can even compare pupils in the class with each other; you can even compare progress if you like doing the maths (few Humanities teachers do).

But this is incomplete. The above test is fine if you are assessing raw facts and data, and you're not interested in anything else. But schools are interested in other things, and you should be too. You can safely ignore the debate that has raged in education for decades about what is more important to teach the students: facts or skills. Some educationalists feel that facts are paramount, and students will develop good thinking skills on their own by manipulating and reflecting upon these facts. Other educationalists rage and storm against this traditional approach, and believe that thinking skills are the key task of the teacher; mere facts are simply the objects that the skills operate upon and, although important, are of secondary importance to the ability to discern, judge and estimate. And the long winter nights roll in.

You teach both. Once you're more confident with your teaching, you can get your knickers in a twist about such crucial matters that seem to possess educationalists and ministerial policy makers, and nobody else. Thinking skills require facts to operate upon; facts are useless, perhaps even impossible to hold, without a capacity to evaluate and contextualize. Play safe, and teach them both; mainly because it's impossible to do one without the other.

So you're trying to teach both: both things they need to know, and things they need to do. How do you monitor and track that little lot? Simple. In order to teach both, the best advice is to get them doing both. Repetition is a centuries old device for memorising facts. If you're trying to learn a skill, you have to do the skill yourself. Examples of skills that you might have to teach them are:

◆ evaluate if an argument is justified or not
◆ thread a sewing machine
◆ drill a hole in a piece of plastic
◆ discern the causes of the Vietnam war

◆ swimming in a circle
◆ playing a scale

There's nothing for it; you have to get them doing these things if you want to get them to improve. There's only so much you can tell them before they need to get their hands dirty[5]. That, in one of the simplest nutshells I can imagine, is the basis of teaching. You wonder why so many people try to mystify it when it's as simple as that.[6]

If you want an A-level philosophy student to get better at comparing good reasons for holding beliefs with bad reasons for holding beliefs, get her to look at some beliefs with both types of justification, point out their relative merits (and tell her why) and then get her to try the same exercise with a range of other beliefs, or her own beliefs. Then you give feedback, and the process starts again. You can make the process more complicated by getting her to criticize your arguments or assumptions, then that becomes another skill you're teaching, and you follow the same process. No matter how many ways you look at it, this is the role of the educator, and has been for many, many hundreds of years. As you progress and learn as a teacher, you will encounter many kinks and complications in this very simple model, and you may generate some of these kinks and criticisms yourself. But the paradigm remains good. Sail your boat by this star, and you'll never be lost at sea.[7]

Assessments

So now you're clear what it is you're doing: you're not just walking into a room and telling them stuff, you're teaching them information/skills, and how to use them. Hopefully along the way you're also enthusing them, and incidentally teaching them how to be adults at he same time. Not too much to ask, is it? Perhaps you can sort of the Israel/Palestine conflict while you're at it, and square a circle.

---

[5] Which, you might have noticed, is how teaching works too. I'm hoping that you haven't noticed it yet, or if you have, that you've bought this book already.

[6] Although I suspect there's a fairly large industry behind them, relying on the idea that teaching is an enormously complex and arcane skill. It's not; it's as uncomplicated as the ambitions of an X-Factor hopeful. What it *does* require is dedication, stamina, patience and courage.

[7] Arrr.

How do you assess? Fortunately, others have walked this path before you, and there is an enormous world of resources to assist you. The school you join should be marking and assessing to a particular framework already, so the first thing you need to do (perhaps more successfully than I did) is find out how they already do it.

In Key Stages 1–3 there are usually loosely defined levels of achievement for each subject; these are called attainment levels, and there might be several or many of them. Rather than being a mark out of twenty, or some other numerical equivalent, an attainment level is reached when a student can do the sorts of things described in the attainment level. For example, in Religious Studies, level three is reached when a student can: 'make links between beliefs and sources, including religious stories and sacred texts (level 3).'[8] So when you have evidence that the pupil is capable of doing this, then you can mark the student as having reached attainment level three. These levels proceed from zero all the way up to attainment level 8, which is broadly speaking the highest category of ability that most students at the end of Key Stage 3 will attain (there will always be exceptions to this, of course, and you need to be alert for the rare exceptionally gifted child).

The levels (or statutory National Curriculum Levels as they are called) apply from Key Stage 1 to the end of Key Stage 3. In Key Stage 4, students are assessed against the benchmarks of their GCSE subjects, which are publicly examinable. These subjects will have an agreed marking scheme, i.e. a universal way of giving the student's work a grade, which is usually expressed as an 'A', a 'B', a 'C' etc. This way of marking, along with the National Curriculum levels, are meant to be a national benchmarking system, where students from a school in the Orkney Isles can be compared with students from an inner-city school in Liverpool. It is designed to improve standards by establishing a universal system of comparison, thereby enabling external assessors to make judgments about relative efficiency, under-achievement, etc.

Compare this to a race around a football pitch. The person who wins doesn't have to beat a certain time; they only have to come first. Success, and measuring that success, is a relative process. This is fine, but it doesn't enable you to compare those runners with other runners, who may have raced up and down a hill. Setting every pupil similar milestones of achievement enables national evaluation to take place.

---

[8] Source: http://curriculum.qcda.gov.uk/key-stages-1-and-2/assessment/assessmentofsubjects/assessmentinreligiouseducation/index.aspx

The theory is that, on average, most students of a certain age range should have reached a certain target level by a certain point in their academic career. If a student enters Year Nine, and is still only achieving level 3 on their assessments, then flags of concern are hoisted, and support can be offered (hopefully before this stage, of course). These targets are worked out using a set of algorithms based on national performance for hundreds of thousands of pupils, so the idea is that the levels are broadly appropriate as guidelines for achievement, in the same way that most child development specialists would expect a toddler to be making their first steps round about the 12 month mark.

It's a much harder process of marking than before, but it requires teachers to be sensitive to the student and to their own topic and its indigenous skills. It requires us to make value judgments, and to be professionals, which can't be a bad thing.

At this stage I must point out that the use of levels in the classroom is far from universally approved of in teaching. Many people see it as an unnecessary complication, as a way of shoehorning learning into an unrealistic model. Some say that the levels are controversial, overlap too much, and stagger under a weight of assumptions about thinking and learning that ultimately render them useless. Not me, of course. In the meantime, you'll be expected to use them, so get your head around them ASAP.

Assessment for learning

This is currently a very popular technique in assessment. It covers many topics, but broadly speaking it encourages teachers to drive students forward in their learning, rather than merely telling them how they are doing. A common mark in my book from when I was a student would be '15/20. Well done'. That's nice, but all it's told me is what I got out of twenty, and how the teacher feels about it. I then, of course, rush over to my pals and say, 'What did you get?' The number is all.

Assessment for learning discourages this; it asks teachers to forego giving grades and numbers to marking (I know, it just feels wrong doesn't it?) and instead give the student two main pieces of information:

♦ What is good about the piece of work?
♦ How can they improve it

Homework

Marking a class set of books will take you an hour, easy, and probably more. If you just want to 'flick and tick' every page, giving a book a few Nike swooshes as you go along, then fine, but all you've done is tell the student you've seen the book. That's not by itself without value, because at least the student knows they have to maintain a certain standard of quality and amount of work, but it doesn't do much more.

Your school will probably have a homework policy. Find out what it is. If it requires you to set weekly homework, then play smart in order to save yourself from self-destructing. When you mark, mark properly, with comments and way forward. This is an invaluable way of communicating with the pupil on a personal level, and enables you to keep teaching beyond the classroom. The more advanced the student, the more detailed the advice you will need to give in order to push them harder. In fact, many teachers have problems with this with the older, more able pupils, especially at A-level, where sometimes in order for the student to progress further the teacher needs to be giving them problems and challenges that a first year undergraduate might face. It's tough, but that's the game. Thankfully, most students won't need that kind of challenge, but as a teacher you need to get away a bit from 'I'm pleased' and into the realms of 'Have you considered another opinion here?' or 'Your workings in this equation don't follow; look and see where it breaks down.' The advice you give needs to be practical, it needs to be clear, and it needs to be achievable by the student.

Praise is a very valuable tool in marking. With some students, the comments you make might be the longest conversation you have with them, particularly if they are quiet and of middle ability (and therefore neither grab your attention due to poor behaviour, nor stun you with their exceptionality. Such kids can be ignored all too easily by teachers). It can be the perfect chance to say something good to them that they might not get to hear in the classroom. Many pupils don't think it's cool to get any approval from the teacher in front of their mates, while secretly they love the praise you give them.

Of course, this must be balanced with severity and being straight-forward. You can still say something direct and critical like 'this isn't good enough'. God forbid we should lose the faculty of saying that something is terrible when it's terrible. But remember that most judgements, even very critical ones, can be expressed in such a way that the student understands without offence. Even bad news can be delivered well.

Don't lose sight of your work/life balance. Your head will melt if you try to mark thoroughly every book every week. Here are some suggestions about staying sane:

1. Set homework that doesn't require extensive marking:
    ◆   For example: get them to revise the meanings of five key words for the next lesson's starter. You check if it's been done by the quality of their verbal answers. Traffic lights are a good strategy with this: you give all students three coloured cards (green/amber/red) to indicate three different answers. Then you set a question and get them to respond using the cards. It's quick, and a good visual way to see if they understand.
    ◆   Research a news story about a topic you provide.
    ◆   Bring in a household product that shows good design or lettering.
2. Set homework that the students can mark (peer marking):
    ◆   This is when the student comes to the lesson prepared for their starter activity. The student performs the starter (perhaps ten questions about the life of Martin Luther King, or famous volcanoes). Then their book is passed to their neighbour, who marks the quiz, scores it then passes it back. This approach works best for factual recall, but is still a useful (and efficient) way to have work marked.
    ◆   This task can be done on a higher level. Set the students an examination-style essay question, and when they bring it in, you can have one of their peers mark it using clear marking criteria as instructed by yourself. This is one of the most powerful teaching tools you can use: when students (particularly students at Key Stage 4 and 5) are marking each others' work, using syllabus mark schemes, then they really start to get involved in learning about how to improve their own work.
3. Set large projects:
    ◆   Not every school has a weekly homework requirement. In fact, many schools regard it as didactic and slightly oppressive. Many schools have turned to longer, larger projects that the students have several weeks to complete, and which require more research, preparation and better execution.

My schedule said we had to do Differentiation. Some of the kids were defined as having Special Educational Needs (SEN) which covered a range of symptoms and sins, but usually flagged up some specific difficulty they had with learning (like dyslexia, for instance) or behaviour (like Attention Deficit Hyperactive Disorder, where the kid finds it hard to sit still, pay attention and in general learn). Sometimes I wondered what qualified for classification as SEN and what didn't: I saw one kid who had 'anger management problems' who was allowed to leave the classroom to count backwards from twenty whenever he started to get the red mist. Was that a condition? Or a symptom? I wondered about it then, and continue to do so.[9]

I asked a few teachers about differentiation. They looked amused.

'They're all thick,' one of them said. What do you want to go making work for yourself for?'[10]

'Pitch the lesson to the middle kids – that's most of them. And have a worksheet handy for the stupid ones; fill in the blanks and whatnot.'

'What do I do about the ones in my class that don't speak any English?' I asked. I regularly had one or two kids in each lesson who were here as refugees – principally Kurds, Serbs or Bangladeshi – who didn't have a word of the Queen's. I had no idea what life looked like through their eyes, although I sympathized with them. And I had no idea how to tackle them.

'Are they disturbing the class?' my advisor asked. I assured him they weren't; they just sat there looking out of the window, or, rarely, talking to their fellow refugees.

'Not your problem then,' he said. 'I suppose you could give them something to colour in.' Something told me that wasn't the best use of a kid's time.

'Don't we have translators for them?' I asked. As far as I could see, the only thing those kids should have been doing was learning English, as a springboard to access everything else.

'I think we have a couple. One's off sick this week. The other one works in the Internal Exclusion Unit.' In other words, the kids were stuffed unless they got lucky and they had an assistant who could interpret for them. The poor sods.

'What about the brainy kids, though?' I wasn't giving up with this differentiation lark. My book said I had to master it. The advice I got wasn't any cheerier; in fact, there was even more of an edge to it.

---

[9] Most Monday mornings I struggle to get out of bed at 6.30. I have decided I have Toxic Employment Allergy. Can I get a receipt for that? Thanks.

[10] And if he wasn't worried about ending a sentence with a preposition, then I wasn't going to be either.

'Who cares about them? They're doing OK already. Why on Earth would you want to worry about them – it's the ones that are struggling we need to focus on, to get them up to the same level as everyone else.' One other teacher at least offered this crumb: 'Give them something extra at the end once they've finished – maybe a question that they need to write an essay for. Or a poem,' she said as an afterthought. I suspected that a lot of what I was supposed to be learning would be an afterthought.

Special educational needs

All kids are special aren't they? But, as someone once said, 'If everyone's special, then no one is.'[11] We could argue that every child has unique needs, but if we did that we'd be here all day feverishly writing thirty different lesson plans for every class, every lesson, so I'll pass, thanks. By Special Educational Needs we mean students who perform so far from the average ability that they are judged to require some form of special provision. This could of course by definition include Gifted and Talented Pupils, but in practice it refers to students who are either significantly below the mean ability of the school population, or who have specific learning and behavioural problems that make teaching and learning more difficult.

It is undoubtedly true that many children in your classrooms will present unusual challenges to you teaching, and them learning. The question is: what do you do in order for both to happen? First of all, what kind of Special Educational Needs will you encounter?

Specific Learning Difficulties (SpLD). This is when a student has one particular aspect of their learning impeded in some way; they may be extremely poor at spelling, or their handwriting may be utterly illegible, but in all other respects their abilities may seem within normal ranges.

Emotional, Social and Behavioural Difficulties (EBD, ESBD). This is a large catch-bag of behavioural problems. This could mean anything from a regular chair-chucker to the child who refuses to go into the swimming pool because of body anxieties. Again, because these behaviours are on a continuum, the distinction between everyday

---

[11] That charming piece of glass-half-emptiness was coined by *Syndrome*, the villain from Pixar's *'The Incredibles'*. Not sure if I legally have to credit imaginary beings with quotes, but better safe than sorry.

anxiety or shyness, for example, and extremely withdrawn behaviour is often subjective.

English as an Additional Language(EAL). Obviously this isn't a disability in the conventional sense, but it is clearly a disadvantage in an English-speaking classroom. The teacher needs to be aware of how to reach these pupils in a meaningful way. Many extremely bright students can languish in a Babel-like Hell because they don't understand enough of what's going on around them. If they misbehave, it may be because they have nothing else to do, so be very careful how you perceive these children.

Other issues. There is a range of other problems that children might face, such as dyslexia, that are often deeply misunderstood by teachers. To find out more, speak to your **Special Educational Needs Coordinator (SENCO)**. Best acronymic job title ever (after Assistant Head Of Learning[12]). They are responsible for a range of school provisions, of which you should be aware of three aspects: the SEN register, Teaching Assistants, and Individual Education Plans.

The SEN register. This is a whole school document identifying pupils who have any special needs that you as teacher need to be aware of. It is essential that you familiarize yourself with this list, particularly in relation to the classes that you will be teaching. A Hell of remorse and shame awaits you if you spend twenty minutes shouting down a pupil for not starting his work, until you find that he only speaks Armenian. This register will be your springboard for differentiation.

Teaching Assistants. The SENCO is responsible for ensuring the school meets its responsibilities for providing Teaching Assistants to pupils who need them more than most. They timetable and assign the assistants across the curriculum and timetable, and should inform you of who and what kind of support you and your classes will receive. That's the plan anyway. Make sure you introduce yourself to the SENCO, and discuss any special needs that you might have. [13]

---

[12] You do the maths.

[13] I don't mean if you need extra time in exams, or a scribe or something. I mean, if you want to give the SENCO any input about what classroom provision you need.

Individual Education Plans. Does what it says on the tin: a pupil-specific advice sheet to assist teachers with helping the named pupils to learn. They will usually identify any problems the pupil has, and suggest ways forward in order to enable their access to the lesson.[14]

One of our boys was caught standing on a bus shelter, peeing on the people below. There was a boy who was a compulsive masturbator – perhaps not unusual for his age, but he stood out from the rest by doing it in class. He did it once and the teacher threw his jacket over the offending tender member and said, 'Is that all you've got?' Great serve; jacket ruined, of course.

I think it's worthwhile mentioning how hard it is to get to know names on your first placement, particularly if like me, names quite literally vanish from your head the moment you hear them. Now, if I'd been sensible and had something like a seating plan (I'd heard of them) then I might have been able to learn them gradually. But because I like a challenge/was an idiot, I struggled on with connecting faces to names and hoped for the best. Of course, it made it next to impossible to learn them all, and led to mayhem whenever pupils realized that I couldn't get them in trouble if I couldn't report who they were, the Machiavellian little monkeys.

Luckily I encountered one great universal leveller – you learn the naughty kids' names in about five minutes; not only are they the principal point of discussion in the staffroom, but you practically walk into them, like enormous walls of naughty. It's quite impossible not to get to know them, because expediency demands that you have a working knowledge of about 25 per cent of them instantly. The only other pupil's name I learned quickly was a girl called – wait for it – Queenelizabeth. Not even Queenie, or Elizabeth, but the two words rolled into one. Her mother had come here from Nigeria and thought to herself, 'Now what's a good English name to help my daughter fit into this new country. Let me think. Hmmm ...'

Getting to know you

As in demonology and the Dark Arts (which sound much cuddlier now that Harry Potter has softened us all up to necromancy), if you know something's name, it gives you power over it. Witness

---

[14] Beware though: sometimes they say helpful things like, 'Try not to challenge him on his behaviour,' or, 'Gets upset if he doesn't get what he wants,' which is hugely helpful. Take the advice with a pinch of salt; it's not written for teachers, it's written for a tutor/student environment.

your impotence as anonymous, unknown children dash through your naughty net, laughing gaily as they dance, just out of your reach.

When you start any school, you'll be haunted by this syndrome, so your job is to nail the names to the floor. The first way to do this is to have a seating plan. Oh, they might groan, but they aren't there to socialize, and you're not there to pander to their desires. So before the lesson starts, map out the room (scrawled tables or computer 3D, it's up to you) and, using a class register, allocate them all seats. If you have time, speak to a teacher who knows the class and get some advice. If you don't, then do something easy and obvious, and put them in tables alphabetically, and in a boy/girl, boy/girl pattern, simply to encourage the disruption of pre-established peer groups, which are still predominantly segregated by gender.

On the first lesson, get them all to stand at the back of the room, get some silence, and then call them to tables one by one. There might be a few clowns who take the mickey by pretending to be someone they're not[15] but once they've all sat down, you can tell them to get their planners out and put them on the desks, where you can check names. No planners? Get their other books out. You'll find something. Worried this might make you look like a hard-ass? Stop worrying. It's good if they think you're a hard-ass. It doesn't mean you have to be unpleasant. In this, as in all things, you can be mannerly, respectful and civil. Just don't smile.

I was walking across an empty playground, when I spotted a lone student hiding behind some stairs. He kissed his teeth at me and walked away. I did the obvious thing and followed him. 'Did you hear me?' I said.

'Go f**k yourself man,' he replied over his shoulder, still sucking his teeth loudly. I wasn't having that, so I chased him around the playground in an absurd, humiliating conga for about five minutes before I gave up. What, did I hope he would herd himself into the Head's office?

A few days later I spotted him, explained what the problem was to a senior teacher, and he was dragged to meet me. He said, 'Sorry,' like it was made of razor blades and I said, 'No problem,' like I meant it. Nothing else happened.

He did exactly the same to a senior member of staff the next day, and was excluded for two weeks.

I was learning lessons too.

---

[15] Which as every Disney Princess knows, is something you should *never* do.

Don't smile?

This has to be dealt with, because it is one of the most common pieces of teacherly advice given and remembered, so as with any grand tradition or legend, it at least demands the reverence of seniority. You've heard the adage not to smile before Christmas. Is it true? Actually, mostly yes. I've already spoken about the teacher persona, and the need to conduct yourself with seriousness, gravity and dignity. If you meet a new class and you give them any indication whatsoever that you're Coco the Friendly Teacher, then they will mug you like a drunk in Soho. I mean it. Even the nice kids like a bit of sport. You don't have to be rude (in fact, never do), but you're not there to make them feel all tingly. If you can pull off being serious and professional for a few months (yes, that can mean until Christmas, ho-ho-ho) then you'll make them feel something even more important: secure. And they'll start to trust you. And you'll start to become their teacher. If you absolutely have to smile (maybe you're one of those people. Do you know something I don't?) then keep it to a reluctant half smile, like you're Clint Eastwood and you just realized the bad guy is lined up in your sights. Smile like you don't want to. Kids love it, for some reason.

Back to the seating plan

A few final words on the seating plan: it is not Scripture; it is not infallible. If you've accidentally put Lady Blah-Blah next to her homegirl (Man, I be so fly),[16] then move them. It's *your* room, not theirs, and the more things you do to show them that you know this to be the case, the better. Keep separating them until *you're* happy with the set-up in the room, the one optimal matrix where they can learn without distractions.

Given the school's 'challenging' student population[17] it was unsurprising that a number of students got into substantial trouble; although I'd never

---

[16] I only do this to show you how awful it sounds. You are not P. Diddy. If you are, you should be ashamed of yourself. Never speak in Jafaican, Urban Dialect, Mockney, or Transatlantic Ghetto, unless you want the kids to evaporate in embarrassment. Think: Uncle dancing at wedding.

[17] 'Challenging' was a word I heard more and more as I went along. It replaced 'rude', 'confrontational' and 'mental' as adjectives of choice to describe degrees of loopiness and violence.

been anywhere near it at my own school, I gathered that being expelled was the nuclear option for really naughty students. These days it was described as 'excluded', presumably because it had a softer edge to it.[18] Inclusion demanded that children shouldn't be chucked out of schools except in exceptional circumstances, and instead kept in mainstream schools until the day they died, apparently. As a halfway house to an external exclusion (where the pupil was shown the door for a set period), an internal exclusion involved the student being taught in school in a separate area, away from their peers, usually in a more tutorial format that lent itself to a personal, one-to-one experience. There they could still learn within the boundaries of the school institution, and – it was hoped – be re-educated socially in order to re-integrate with the larger school community at some point. That, as they say, was the theory.

I visited the Internal Exclusion Unit, as it was called. It was one of the newer branches of the school, and it looked bloody beautiful, I was shocked, I thought I'd entered another school through a magical wardrobe The rooms were gleaming and new, the desks were irregular rhombuses, and the place swarmed with earnest staff and confused, surly-looking teenagers who looked stunned and passive inside the clean lines of the brightly lit engine of modernity. It was strange to come from my tired, Soviet Humanities block to this primary-coloured temple of the future; it was strange to think how much money had been made available to remedy the behaviour and learning of the very worst of the pupils, and how little had been spent elsewhere. Even the music department was so poor that the only band they could form was a Steel Drum band, because that's pretty much all they had for the kids to use (plus some xylophones, which were missing so many teeth I assumed they had been fighting with the tambourines).

The teacher persona

Who are you? This is something that probably doesn't furrow many peoples' brows after the age of seventeen or so, unless you're having a mid-life crisis or you navel-gaze professionally. Who has the time to consider existential introspection when bills have to be paid? As someone once observed: there's not a lot of people taking time off work with stress in the Serengeti Desert. But this is actually a valid

---

[18] Perhaps they should call it 'Involuntary Vacation' or something, in case anyone confuses it with a punishment of some sort and gets offended and the sky falls in.

INCLUSION

question to ask when you become a teacher, and not just a pointless, middle-class exercise in narcissism.

Why is it so important? Because we act out different roles depending on the situation we find ourselves in: we act and speak one way when we're with our employers, another with our grandmother, and another with the people next to you on the bus. I'll share a secret with you; in my private life, I have been known to swear, crack 'edgy' jokes,[19] laugh at others' misfortune, dismiss people's dreams offhand, and walk about with my shirt hanging out. I do not, however, do this in a classroom. 'Fake!' I hear you cry. Of course it's not. It's simply presenting the side of me to the students that will help me teach, and that they need in order to learn. I talk to a lot of new teachers who are worried about what they should do and what they should say in certain situations in the classroom and beyond. 'I wish I was like Teacher X,' they sigh, 'He always knows what to do. Sometimes the kids ask me things, and I have no idea how to answer them.'

The difficulty for anyone giving advice about how to respond is that I can give an infinite series of responses and tactics, but it doesn't help the teacher beyond that one instance. What they really need to do is work on their teacher persona, and settle exactly who it is they see themselves as in the classroom.

Let me tell me who you're probably not: you're probably not the non-teacher persona you present to family, friends and colleagues. If you walk into a classroom and act like yourself, be it friendly, jokey or chatty, then the kids will instantly mark you out as a sucker. They won't see you as what you should be, which is an authority figure. You need to step into a personality when you step into the classroom, Hell, when you step into the school. This does not mean being horribly false, or in some way fake. It does mean that you need to bring out your inner teacher. Personally, I ask myself: What would Sean Connery do? Or what would Fonzie do? Or what would any mature, authoritative role model do? Best of all, you should imagine what you would do if you were as confident, professional and authoritative as you'd like to be. Imagine it. Eventually you'll be it, and it won't be an act anymore.

You will need to be yourself, as I said; there is no point being someone you are completely not. But if you can't muster up a little gravity and mastery, then perhaps you're in the wrong career. The classroom needs leaders, and like it or not, it's you. You need to be:

◆ confident
◆ calm
◆ slow to react to provocation
◆ fair
◆ reasonable
◆ determined
◆ consistent

---

[19] Nothing involving 'my mate Chalky' or anything of that nature, I stress.

◆ prepared
◆ mannerly

There are dozens of other adjectives you could add here, but these will do for now. You can still be humorous, kind, stern, slightly manic, or any other personality type, but you need to be able to access the kinds of characteristics I've listed above. The list is not exhaustive, and certainly isn't prescriptive. But if you skip too many of these characteristics too often, you'll start to find yourself in trouble. Too nervous? They'll smell fear and pounce. Not fair? They'll seethe with dislike. Unprepared? They'll think you're a clown.

There's a word that encapsulates all of the above, and more: adult. You have to be the adult in the room. You may have just come through a BEd; you may be older than the sixth formers by a handful of years; regardless, you are the adult in the room. Remember that to children, anyone older than twenty five is essentially geriatric, and listens to the Beatles. I mean it. To them, you are the grown-up, you are in Mum and Dad's category. If you're not ready to act like the adult, then don't be a teacher. If you want to be really chummy with them, then get a life. They're not your chums, unless you present Blue Peter. They're also not your audience; don't enter teaching thinking that you're a crazy entertainer who'll charm them into learning. You're not. Go and work in Butlins, jackanapes.

The fact that I need to say this might sound odd, but then, society has changed a lot. Just as many children have acquired the belief that they are entitled to the rights of adulthood (see: cigarettes, alcohol, swearing, sex, etc.), so too many adults refuse to imagine that they might need to grow up at some point. Men my age were, in my grandfather's era, becoming grandfathers. I regularly meet parents in their forties who play computer games and dress like teenagers, reluctant to help little Jimmy with his homework because they (the parents) want to go out clubbing. Far be it from me to criticize others on their lifestyle choices,[20] but there has been an immense blurring of the boundaries between adulthood and childhood, and many people enjoy a period of extended infancy well into parenthood.

That may be fine, or it may not. But don't dare step into the classroom until you are certain of these facts: you are an adult; they are children; you are entitled to train them to become adults; your opinion in the classroom is immensely more important than theirs; what *you* say goes; if they disobey you, then *they* have done

---

[20] I wouldn't *dream* of it.

wrong. Far, far too many teachers wrack themselves with doubt and indecision, worrying if they have done the right thing, or if they've let the children down by not listening to them enough, or for raising their voices, or for wondering if they really are terrible teachers after all.

Don't worry if they resent you at first. Don't mind if they aren't gazing at you adoringly from the carpet. Worry about them learning; that's why you're paid the big bucks. To give them an education. To lead them. To guide them into adulthood. To every single one of my classes I say the same thing:

'I am your teacher; that is the most important job in my life; I take it very seriously. Without knowing you, I care a great deal about what happens to you. My particular concern is that you learn as much as possible to prepare you for your lives. Because I care so much, I'll do whatever I can to make sure you get that education. That means that if anything – or anyone – stops me from doing my job, then I'll take steps to remove that problem. I care so much about your education that I'm prepared to be tough on you, to give you the best learning I can. Does anyone have a problem with that?'

If any clown tries to goof off with that last comment, they've done me a favour and flagged up who I need to work on first. Oh, and they get half an hour with me that day, and a phone call home, to ask their parents if they can help me re-educate their son. That's who you are. You're the teacher.

Reuben burst into my room like a cannonball, parking the lesson instantly.

'Reuben, get yourself sat down. You're late,' I said. Stating the obvious was, at least, uncontroversial. But Reuben wasn't feeling conciliatory. He scowled at me, offended by my slight when he was entertaining everybody.

'Yeah blud, chill the f**k out,' he said.

'Leave the lesson, Reuben,' I said. 'Now.'

'You can't tell me to leave the lesson. Who are you? Who are you?' he said, stepping up nicely and, I might add, getting interestingly close to my personal space. He started to stalk around the room like a clown, shouting his pea-brained head off.

'La! La! La!' he repeated, over and over. 'La! La! La!' I asked him to leave several times, but I was losing my cool; I could feel it. Weeks and weeks of this kind of thing was eating away at me.

'For God's sake, Reuben, just shut up and get out of the room!' I shouted. He pounced on it.

'Shut up! Shut up! You can't tell me to shut up! Teachers can't tell us to shut up! Everyone – did you hear that – you back me up; stupid waste just told me to shut up! No, you shut up, man!'

I had pressed a trigger; they didn't like it if you said shut up. I got into a face-to-face argument with him, where I at least kept my head and just kept telling him to get out, and he barged around the room showing that he thought nothing of me or my lesson. This went on for ten minutes. I asked a girl to go get some assistance (I was still teaching completely solo, and had been since my first week); she refused to go.

A small, pretty girl put her hand up. I mention it purely because of the contrast it made with the long, ugly scar that travelled down her face. Eventually, half an hour into the lesson, and without a shred of work being done by anyone, I noticed her, me still mid-argument.

'Yes, Carli?' I said, wondering what she had to say at this juncture.

'It's just …' she looked shy. 'Do you have any work for us to do? We're bored.' She didn't say it with a sneer. She wasn't taking the mickey. She just wanted to get on with something, while I spent all my time and energy exhausting myself against Reuben and his self-destruction. I felt exactly as ashamed of myself as I should. There were twenty-five kids in that classroom, and I was going toe-to-toe with one of them, and to Hell with the rest. I grabbed a passing teacher from the corridor and had Reuben taken out. Then I finished the lesson.

In the staffroom, a colleague told me about Carli. Her father, an alcoholic and addict, had smashed a bottle into his daughter's face for reasons only he knew; he was long gone, anyway. The mother, also an alcoholic, threw Carli out every morning and told her not to come back until it was dark. So every day she went to a friend's house, whose parents had a more nurturing idea of parenthood, who fed her and let her wash. After school she went back with her friend and did her homework, and ate. When it was dark enough she crept back home, and hoped that her mother was drunk enough to be comatose. This, every day for years. In between breakfast and nightfall she came to school and worked as hard as she could, in every lesson she could.

One day, before I waved a tearful goodbye to the school, I spoke to her at the end of the lesson. I told her how proud I was of her hard work. Without referring to her background – how do you introduce something like that? – I asked how she managed to stay so cheerful and work so hard even when there was so much chaos going on around her. She answered without a pause.

'Because I want out,' she said. 'Because I want things to be better.'

It took years for me to realize what she had told me.

What I should have done was set the class a straightforward activity that I wouldn't need to supervise closely, e.g. book work. I knew the class was hard, and should have been ready to get the class rolling and then brace myself for the mentals. A pity it took a fourteen-year-old girl to point that out to me.

Safety

As a teacher in a school of any size, you will come face to face with other peoples' lives; some of those lives will be dysfunctional, or marbled with tragedy, violence and misery. You may even have had firsthand experience of such matters yourself. You only need to scratch at the veneer of polite society for the paint to flake off to reveal darker shades beneath. As you stand in front of a class, you can be reasonably sure that some of the people you're looking after will go back to homes less supportive or stable than you would dream possible. As you face an assembly you can be certain of it.

As a teacher you are in loco parentis; this means you are deemed to stand in place of the guardian or parent. Imagine they were your own children, or members of your family. How do you keep them safe?

◆ First of all, remember your teacher persona. Make the behaviour expectations clear, which will automatically (one would hope) include basic rules about how and when pupils move around the room and interact with each other. For example, pupils should request permission to leave their seats and the room.

◆ Make sure that pupils are explicitly aware of how they conduct themselves socially: hands up, no shouting, no throwing, etc. Basic stuff, but utterly essential. I mean, I can't imagine there exists a child so slow that they believe the proper way to pass scissors is by throwing them like shuriken, but you never know.

◆ Only leave the room in an emergency. This needs to be read in context; if your cupboard is directly adjacent to your workspace then it's not ideal, but possibly permissible. If you need to leave the room for a legitimate reason (for example to speak to a pupil who has been parked outside your room) then keep the door open with a foot or a chair so the student space is still available to you. I heard of a teacher who left her classroom when an OfSTED inspector was observing her ... to go get some stuff from the boot of her car in the street outside the school. 'Can you just watch them for a minute?' she asked the boggling inspector, whose finger never hovered above 'fail'[21] for a second. It's not often I sympathize with an inspector.

◆ Don't organize/permit any activities that the students might find dangerous – genuinely dangerous, that is; I weep with frustration when I hear about children being forbidden from engaging in

---

[21] Sorry, I should say 'unsatisfactory'. It means 'fail', though.

'risky' activities – I seem to remember playing rugby in Winter at my school, and that was bloody risky. There is risk in all aspects of life, and the desire to wrap children in cotton wool is detestable.

A couple of months of this, and I was starting to give up the spirit. I went home every night and wondered if it was worth it, lying on my bed and staring at the ceiling. Every week I went back to the Institute to talk to other teachers, some of whom had hairy stories of their own, but none of them with the relentless repetition or severity of mine. I was beginning to think I'd been put in the worst school in England. Nobody else had a kid w*nking in their classrooms, and some of them even seemed to be teaching in the 1940s. Envious and depressed, the Christmas break didn't come soon enough.

I had been assured that after Christmas I would see a difference in the children's behaviour, on the basis that they would be amazed to see me return. This in turn was underpinned by the assumption they had that new teachers would be gone in a matter of days; most children assumed that new teachers were on temporary supply, which meant they had carte blanche to terrorize them until their corduroy trousers melted. Coming back after a term break implied that you were there for the duration (even if my placement would only extend for another few months). And so it was, at least partially – the behaviour went from impossible and soul-destroying to merely chaotic and cruel. Some of the children started to comply regularly, although outbreaks of anarchy were still common. They were also difficult to handle because everything I tried to control the lessons wasn't working; I'd tried to set detentions – they never showed up; I'd varied my lessons, my tone of voice – ignored; I talked through problems with them, and attempted to engage them sympathetically – nothing. I tried to make them laugh – less than nothing. I tried to make them scared – nothing. It was all nothing. I was nothing.

Just about the only thing I did do that worked was tell stories; I'm not good at telling stories around a dinner table, but it was impossible to live and work in Soho for eight years and not pick up some funny tales, grotesques or comedies of errors, so whenever a subject seemed appropriate, I would link it to something I had done, or witnessed from between my fingers. It seemed to have an effect. They listened, and sometimes I even got a laugh; I always got questions afterwards, and sometimes got asked for more. It was an enormous relief, just occasionally, to have their interest rather than their disdain. But I had my content to get through, so I always put the stories away when I wished I could have carried on all day.

Child protection

As part of your responsibility to look after the pupils, you may come across situations when pupils reveal, deliberately or not, serious dangers to their mental or physical well being in their personal lives. This is as important as it gets. Teachers aren't social workers, but we're human beings, and quite apart from the duty we have to each other as humans, we also have the duty of being in loco parentis. It's also one of the most incredibly delicate things you'll ever have to deal with; even as a trainee teacher you may hear or see something or be told something that causes you grave concern, such as:

- unusual bruises or cuts that can't be explained easily, or that appear regularly
- a normally exuberant child becoming more and more withdrawn
- an overheard conversation about underage students discussing sexual practices
- witnessing a pupil smoking
- a pupil waits behind to tell you she's been raped

These are rare enough to be unusual, and common enough to be something you might possibly come across. I have encountered all of these. Your options can seem bewildering. Fortunately every school should (and legally does) have guidelines in place for these circumstances.

First of all, every school should have a designated member of staff who is responsible for looking into these issues, the Child Protection Officer. This person should be your first port of call. They need to be informed of your concern as soon as possible, even to the extent of cancelling your next lesson. If it could mean the difference between a child going home to be sexually assaulted, and action being taken to prevent that, your priorities suddenly become clear. The CPO will take your statement and then make a judgement about the immediate course of action; usually it will be to contact further social services, such as the police or the social work department, to see what advice they give. Sometimes it involves immediate action; sometimes the police are involved from the word go. Sometimes children are taken into care that day. Often they're not; often the only actions taken are investigations and interviews. Sometimes you make a wrong call and there's no problem. Better safe than sorry.

If you are approached by a student who then makes a disclosure, the best advice is to listen sympathetically and express concern. You mustn't guarantee anonymity, so make that clear at the start – they need to know that you're going to take this a step further. Be sympathetic, but always try to be fair – after all, allegations can be false as well as true, and unless you hear both sides of the story, you're not in a position to judge. So try to be supportive and sympathetic without being judge, jury and executioner. Let others decide the veracity of the story. Just be honoured that someone trusts you enough to talk to you about something that could be tearing them apart. Once you've made a statement to the CPO, you may be asked to write a statement, or give evidence at a later date to other civil services.

As my time in Purgatory wound up, we all reconvened at college for a short period to discuss the looming second placement.

Mine was a real beauty; a complete contrast to the first, and such a sudden gear change I nearly died from the bends. The staff room looked like the breakout area of Microsoft HQ, lined with PCs and immaculate lines of laminate tables; it was also silent and serious. Teachers worked there, rather than gossiped about how awful the kids or the senior staff were. The dining hall was tidy and efficient, serving food that was edible, desirable even. The quads were leafy and ordered, and in the summer students sat there for lessons while they discussed poetry or physics. It was an entirely agreeable place to be. For one thing, there was no sense of threat or danger, and the children actually held doors open for teachers as they approached, which led me to pinch myself frequently. It took me a week to stop flinching every time a student approached.

It was one of the first Specialist Schools in the UK; a beacon school; an ICT test-bed school, with £2.5 million invested in its computer systems. Awards fell like skittles before its majesty.

It was, in other words, terrifying.

6 | Be the inspiration: *Starting to feel like a teacher*

What a difference: the intake was drastically different. Employment was much higher, and with it something was in the air that I hadn't felt for a while: aspiration. The kids there didn't assume that school was pointless, didn't assume that they would end up working the nightshift in the BP garage, didn't imagine their futures would be mirror images of those of their parents. They weren't better, or worse, or smarter, or classier: they just had different aspirations.

My fellow trainees and I quickly formed a tribe, and like any group we huddled in the same area of the enormous staffroom, joking and whispering and comparing notes. After a few days we received a note in our collective pigeonhole:

'It has come to the attention of staff that some members of the trainee cohort have been using the staffroom for social and relaxation purposes; we would like to take this opportunity to remind you that the staffroom is a work area, and not an area for unnecessary talking. We would also like to remind the cohort that no items should be left on desks between academic days; such items will be removed. Thank you for your anticipated cooperation.'

We got the message. Eventually we were told to vacate the staffroom computers 'if a full-time member of staff required it'. Which made our position in the food chain pretty clear.

Staffrooms and other dungeons

The staffroom of any school can be a minefield. They range from the immaculate First Class suites of British Airway departure lounges to something like a teenager's bedroom. Smoking staffrooms are a thing of the past (and already seem impossibly distant and impossible), but unless you distance teach using a webcam, you'll find yourself in one before long. They have at least two utilities: social and occupational.

Some teachers, no matter how busy, seem to find endless pockets of time to natter and vent, and unless you want your dirty laundry to be overheard by everyone in 7M then the staffroom is the only safe place to be. It's important for you as a teacher to be able to get stuff off your chest, sympathize with others and generally realize that you're not entirely alone through your daily routine. The other side of the coin is that the staffroom often acts as the main workspace for colleagues on the odd lessons they have free. Perhaps you can already see a tension between the two endeavours?

Innocent though they may be, there are several reasons why the staffroom is especially important to you as a new teacher. For a start, this is where you will meet most of your colleagues; and where, if you don't meet them, then they will observe you, however obliquely. Of course, you will only be of passing interest to the majority of teachers; their immediate priorities will be to identify if you are directly connected to anything they are connected with. If not, then they will probably stay out of your way, not out of rudeness, but simply through expediency. Some of the friendlier ones may, of course, introduce themselves and ask how you are doing; they may even offer to help in some way. In my experience, teaching is a notoriously supportive profession, probably because we intuitively recognize the need to collaborate.

It's important (and polite) for you to tread carefully in the staffroom. The first few days you should be gently observing how things work: is it a chatty place, covered in crumbs and newspapers? Then go forth and do likewise if you want, being careful not to barge into anyone's conversation. Be friendly, but not too forward, as people (in every walk) prefer strangers to become friends by a gradual process. But don't hang back like the invisible man either – like a high school dance, sometimes you have to make the first approach.

If the room is dignified, organized and spotless, then tread even more carefully; don't clutter up terminals and desk space while you update your Facebook or read the Sun, unless you want a snooty message left in your pigeonhole, which is the teaching equivalent of a horse's head in your bed.

If you are blessed with locker space, then use it as means of not carrying everything about with you. It should also be an emergency deposit for some stationery, paper and nibbles, as no day is complete without some kind of savoury/sweet snack.[1] I found it useful to

---

[1] If you can cope a whole day without some kind or oral recompense then you are either God or Monster.

stash hand wipes, plasters and a change of clothes[2] in here, too. Your pigeonhole, if you have one, should be checked several times throughout the day, because (barring email) it is one of the most common ways to get messages around the school, and saves people hiking around the campus to find you every time they want to tell you that the school Hall is out of action. Empty your pigeonhole every day – it's not a storage space, it's a message space, and less significantly a to-do pile. If you don't have to-do it then move it into your locker, your bag, your filing cabinet, the bin. Stay on top of this kind of stuff, because the paperless office is still as distant as hover boots and light sabres. Paper is still the dominant currency in schools. If we closed them all down, the forests of the world would fall over in shock, and earth would be covered in trees in a fortnight.[3]

Some more good staffroom etiquette:

◆ Buy a mug, and hide it somewhere safe. Make sure it is clearly identifiable. Using other people's mugs is a hanging offence in some schools.[4]

◆ If you bring some biscuits in, share them with people. Don't sit there munching on a packet of Jaffa Cakes while your colleagues sit drooling and wondering how to knock you unconscious.

◆ If you have a spare cake at home, bring it in and leave it in the staffroom, saying, 'This is left over birthday cake (or whatever), and I'll never finish it.' Leaving a note next to it saying it's for everyone also works a charm.[5] It will last about five minutes. If it lasts any longer then you'll know it must be really awful, because teachers will eat anything vaguely cakey as long as it isn't actually moving. This will earn you brownie (ho-ho) points with everyone, and they will know your name ever after. I'm serious; this is a win-win situation. The only other way of getting this much kudos instantly would be by somehow disbanding OfSTED or putting a tenner in everyone's pigeon hole. Cakes are easier. Everyone likes cake.[6]

◆ Pick your rubbish up. That includes papers, books and marking.

---

[2] Don't ask. All I can say is that in my years of teaching, I have found this to be a life saver on at least two occasions.

[3] Schools are like Saruman in that respect

[4] It's actually much more serious than that.

[5] For God's sake put your name to it, or everyone will inhale it. *Why is this cake here?* they'll ask. Worse, perhaps no one will eat it because no one knows if it's for public consumption. And then the janitor will eat it.

[6] *Nice* cake, mind. None of that garage-shop rubbish.

- Don't have long phone conversations.

- Don't use the meagre printer as your means to churn out two hundred worksheets (unless you have no choice); the school will usually have better facilities for bulk printing. Eventually someone will go over to the printer and say in a snooty voice, 'Who is printing off two hundred work sheets on the Kreb's Cycle?' And it'll be you, you shameless cad.

- Wearing headphones and listening to music is a good way of tuning out the drone of conversation. Having cheap headphones that leak out Abba tunes or dirty phat hip-hop is a quick way of making enemies.

- The staffroom is a haven, but it is still a room in which to be professional; openly complaining about other teachers personally is an awful thing to do in a pubic space. So is unnecessary venting and aggression. If you feel like letting it all out … don't. Keep tears, rage and misery to close friends and responsible colleagues. You don't want everyone to think you're the angry one, or the one that's a bit mental.

Still, it was hard to fault the school, even if sometimes it felt a little heavy-handed. Teachers worked hard, and my two mentors were kind and supportive. Again, I was expected to plan and execute lessons pretty much solo from week one, but after my first school I had got pretty used to this. The biggest difference I experienced was that the school was one of the most advanced I'd seen in ICT, which made my mouth water. I love teaching 'naked' (which I'd better explain rapidly means with as little resources as possible). I like the thrill of teaching with nothing but you, the kids and your minds. Books, paper, even boards are just tools, and real teaching can happen without it. But IT can be an enormous boon to a lesson too; video, pictures and sounds can bring foreign cultures alive, and transport the whole world into the classroom. No more grainy black and white pictures in ruined, Jurassic textbooks; life size Buddhas, the pilgrimage to Mecca, the speeches of Martin Luther King Jnr, all in front of their eyes. I love using computers, and I've tinkered with them since Clive Sinclair first made grainy block graphics a reality for every Tron addict in the eighties.

ICT

By now everyone is so hip to the use of computer technology that even the phrase 'computer technology' seems quaint and square. I'm sure that everyone entering a classroom these days is fully conversant with the computer revolution, unless you've started your training at an age beyond forty or so.[7] Even then you'd have to be Amish or something. Interactive Whiteboards, a Battlestar Galactica fantasy when I was a kid, are now standard practice. If there's a school staffroom that doesn't have a bank of computers for teachers to use, then good luck – how are the Shetland Isles? Many teachers now confidently and constantly use computers as integral parts of their lessons and schemes of work. The ubiquitousness of IT in teaching can provide a major lift to the quality of lessons in almost all subjects. Some words of wisdom about the use of technology to assist a lesson:

◆ It's a tool, not an end in itself. If you feel the technology is getting in the way of learning, your teaching or becoming an enormous encumbrance to your lesson planning, then ditch it immediately, or at least rein it in to its proper place. Anything you use in the classroom, from a chalk rubber to a white board, is a tool to aid lessons, nothing more. The greater aim is education. If you find yourself spending all day and night designing lesson resources for the computer, then I commend your dedication; now cool your jets and teach a little bit more naked.[8]

◆ PowerPoint. This is a great way of presenting a lesson, but if you've ever sat through an interminably long presentation as part of your training, or in a professional capacity, you'll understand why people call it 'death by PowerPoint'.[9] If you suspect that showing people slide after slide of brightly coloured text broken up by bullet points is a bit boring, you'd be absolutely right. Kids often treat PowerPoint presentations as enormous widescreen TVs and start to drift off, bathed in a lovely glow as they sit there in the enticing darkness. Keep the slides brief, and break them up with active tasks, otherwise you should consider a career in management training courses held in mid-price hotels.

---

[7] In which case I'LL SPEAK UP. Ho-ho. Perhaps you could get one of the kids to 'log on' to the 'interweb' so that you can 'access' all the 'files'.

[8] The naked teacher – I like that. I think I'll … oh bugger, someone beat me to it.

[9] Capital punishment option in some American states, apparently.

Shall we start with an ice-breaker? Tell the person next to you something about you that no one else knows ...[10]

♦ Get them trained in netiquette.[11] Children all too easily associate computers with relaxation, entertainment and instant, prodigious communication of drivel[12] between themselves and their peers. You have to teach them that computers can be about drudgery and labour as well as pleasure – well, perhaps not, but make it clear to them that if they monkey about playing Flash games and selling their kidneys on eBay then they'll be sitting on the naughty step for the rest of the lesson. Drill this home early on in your relationship with them, or you'll spend the rest of your school career chasing them off Facebook.

♦ Computers are a fantastic tool for research, but they are essentially just an extension of existing resources: text on a screen, no matter how hyperlinked or capable of branching off, is still text, and until we learn how to pipe data directly into their brains, text and speech are the best ways we have of communicating. There is nothing intrinsically superior about asking a pupil to find an article on the net than asking him to find it in a book, so ask yourself if you're utilising IT purely for novelty value, or because it achieves your goals more precisely.

The second teaching placement saw us all more relaxed, slightly more confident about ourselves. The fear of the unknown was over; now we only feared knowns. It could still be fiendishly difficult, but at least we'd been baptized. We were expected to be up and flying by the second placement. The first placement was designed to give us the basics; the second was where we sharpened our knives.

And that was a problem for me. I felt as though I hadn't picked up the basics; I was still a greenhorn. I wasn't sharpening anything, and I felt myself repeating and repeating myself in lessons, although I imagined that somehow I would pick it up as I went along. Clearly that's what everyone else imagined too.

---

[10] To which I always say, 'I love you.' Or 'I hate being here.'
[11] I'm going to Hell just for using that word.
[12] Have you ever read a typical teenage Instant Chat? It makes Bruce Forsyth look profound and spiritual. Sartre was right.

How long does it take to win a class?

Let me just get my ball of string out and measure a piece. There are too many variables here to give you anything the data junkies from the DfE would be satisfied with. You can start off in one school and find that the kids are pretty much onside the day you walk in the class; this usually occurs when they have been pre-groomed by their feeder schools, the existing school behaviour expectations are tight and tightly enforced, or the parental demographic is highly supportive. There are many schools like this. Or you might walk into the school from Hades, and be battling them metre by metre, minute by minute, as I was in my first placement.

So how many and for how long? Here are some good rules of thumb, bearing in mind that they are as flexible as a sixth former's idea of what constitutes a deadline:

◆ If you go in hard with a new class, they will probably give you a honeymoon period, where they're checking you out. For all they know, you might be the Arnold Schwarzenegger of teaching. They are cautious, and sniff you out to see if you carry out your threats. This is a dreadful period, where some teachers get lulled into an appalling sense of false security. A week or two, probably.

◆ Then they show you what they're really like. This is the start of the war of attrition. By now they should know what you expect. By now you should be setting sanctions consistently and fairly.

◆ If you turn up for detentions, or call home when they don't turn up, and you're escalating sanctions up the ladder (one hour: hour and a half; Headteacher's Detention, etc.) then you will enter the real heart of darkness.

◆ After about a term of this you should have seen the easy kids give in quickly as soon as they see you mean business. The tough nuts will remain tough nuts for a while. They've got more stomach for a fight. If you've started in September, by Christmas you might see this.

◆ Once you come back from the Christmas break they will realize that you haven't quit, and that they are going to have to put up with you. This will be your first benchmark. How are they behaving? Keep applying sanctions.

◆ By the end of term two you should only be seriously battling the major hard nuts, and having minor (although probably constant) skirmishes with the pests.

◆ By the end of the year, you should be battling the toughest of the nuts.

I've said 'should' a lot. There is no 'should'. You are neither a failure if it takes longer, nor a success if you walk into total compliance. It will vary on a lot of things: Are you fair? Are you consistent? Do you have a personality that gels with them? Do you scream at them? Do you tell them you hate them? Do you mark their homework? Are your lessons planned well? I emphasize: a well-planned lesson does not guarantee good behaviour, but a disorganized one can contribute to bad behaviour

A year of teaching will be your real first hurdle. The process then continues. Kids resent change and at first, no matter how lovely you are, they will probably show you varying degrees of resentment because you're not the 'real' teacher (by which they mean their old one, or some imagined Platonic ideal). Ignore them; this is entirely natural. You never really reach a destination with good behaviour; it can always improve. Even if they're all sitting quietly and behaving, you will want them to get more proactive, more enthusiastic and more independent. Behaviour management is a process, not a target. It is never achieved.

I no longer felt my guts turn to water at the thought of entering a classroom and being holed up with them for a spell (long spells too – the school ran lessons that went to an hour and a quarter, which at first felt like Narnia time). Behaviour wasn't such a problem either – if any of the kids fell off task it was relatively easy to nudge them back on the table again. But this lulled me into a false sense of security. I thought that my behaviour management had improved significantly because behaviour was better in my classes. But this wasn't the case; they were merely better behaved. As soon as I met a real hard nut, of which there were few, I went to pieces all over again.

There was one girl, a particularly unpleasant brat from a well-off home, who had everything she needed. She was popular, fashionable, slim and extremely smart. She was also catty, cruel and arrogant, like a budget 90210 Prom Queen. She rushed up to every boundary I set, stepped over it and stepped back.

'Why aren't you working?' I would ask her. She would slump on the desk, and I would repeat myself. When she tired of hearing me do this enough, she would say, 'I'm not well,' or 'It's too hard.' Both of these options left the soft-centred teacher at the mercy of his/her own sappiness. Both weren't easy disputes to swat, because to do so would have entailed assuming the student was lying, which is a tough mark to step up to. She ran, I have to say, rings around me. She came late, she truanted, she ignored homework, she talked when she felt like it ... and I did next to nothing, because I didn't know what to do.

'You're an idiot!' she shouted at me, when I'd pushed her too far. By saying that, at least it was clear defiance, and something I could report. She showed me how low-level defiance could be even worse than open aggression or confrontation, because it was corrosive rather than explosive. She also showed me how perfectly intelligent people could be terrible students.

Gifted and talented pupils

There will be, in every school, some exceptionally bright or talented students; statistically, this is very probable, in any population with over a few hundred. OK, so maybe they're not Mozart or a Stephen Hawking, but they will display abilities far beyond those of their contemporaries. For a start, they are usually capable of much harder work than other students, so they often finish earlier, and produce work of higher quality – often, but not always. If they finish first their attention is unoccupied, and some are likely to get up to monkey tricks.

They may also suffer from the dark side of giftedness: arrogance. More able pupils can sometimes be disdainful of people they believe aren't as bright as they are, because of course they've got it all figured out at the age of 11, haven't they? They can be particularly scornful of

'..WHAT... WE CAN'T DO THAT EITHER?
.. SO WHAT CAN WE DO?'

SANCTIONS

newer teachers, especially if the new teachers don't sound confident about their subject matter.

Of course, these are challenges from the teacher's point of view. From the pupil's point of view, if your lessons don't stretch them, or occupy their minds at an appropriate level, then they might easily get bored, switch off, and certainly fail to get as much out of their education with you than they should do. Imagine you were asked to complete an entire book of colouring-in: you, with your degree and everything. You would go mental in about five minutes. That's how many gifted and talented pupils feel in the classroom, the music room and the training field *if* they're not provided for in the classroom.

1. Make sure the work actually challenges the more able in the class. Just because they're working, and they seem occupied or quiet, doesn't mean they're not bored out of their minds and dreaming their escape from the prison they think they're in.
2. This doesn't have to mean tons of extra worksheets and activities for them. As I mentioned in the section on inclusion, think of activities that they can do in different ways. You could allow some more able students to answer a set of questions as one essay, for example.
3. Get more able students to present projects to the class. Get them to share their thoughts with the class during question time in order to provide role models of good practice to the other students, and so they can at least see what's possible.
4. Use them to deepen and broaden debates and thinking for the whole class; ask the less able students an easier question that they are likely to get; praise the student when they (hopefully) get it, and then ask a related, harder question and direct it to a more able student. That way everyone feels involved, successful and challenged appropriately.
5. Expect more from them. This is good advice for every student, but expect fantastic results from more able students. If they produce something beneath what you know they are capable of, push them a little harder.
6. An easy way to think about dealing with gifted pupils is to imagine if they were in the year above the one they presently occupy. That would be a good challenge for most of them. This doesn't mean giving them next year's textbooks (although it could), but thinking about the skills and content they will be reaching for in the next year.

7. To help identify the more able children, there will be a list in every school called the Gifted and Talented register; ask your HOD if he has such a list. He should.

8. Support and encourage them. Many G&T kids feel tremendously disheartened because when they get 'A's, nobody says well done ... but if they get a 'B' once, they get Hell. Basically, all they can do is fail, and they only get attention when they do so. Make sure you're congratulating them if they regularly perform well, and touch base with them to make sure they're not feeling ignored.

9. *Do not*, for God's sake, just give them extra questions to do if they finish first. Most gifted pupils have already worked out that if they finish the task you've set, many teachers will just give them another twenty of the same sums, the same sentences, the same types of questions. Extension work should be different work. It should make them think. Ideally, challenge should be built in to the activities you set them in the first place. If they're regularly finishing before the others, you need to have a look at your own lesson plans.

10. Some more able students respond really well to external projects and extra-curricular challenges, like mini-research projects. This needs to be handled carefully otherwise they smell a rat and see it as extra homework, which it is. See? They're bright. Have a talk with your Gifted and Talented Coordinator for more information about stretching and challenging the more able.

The premises were lovely. I was introduced to my first A-level class, and we would spend afternoons outside on the grassy quadrangle and I would teach like Plato, surrounded by cross legged students in the sunshine. It felt about as far from my first school as it was possible to imagine.

A-level was an eye-opener. It was odd to walk into a class full of students who, for the most part, looked like grown ups, or 'real people' as I like to call them: beards, make-up.[13] Instantly I felt more at ease with them, and I guess that's something that teachers apprehend intuitively or they don't. And the subject – enlightenment philosophers, theodicies and other essentials – was right on my level. I found that planning lessons for these sessions, far from being a tiresome chore, was something I looked forward to. I went to the library to research the topics I had forgotten or never learned, and thought of unusual ways to teach them and novel media that could shine a new light into old corners. In other words, I had found my teaching niche. Those lessons were some of the most enjoyable times I spent in that year or any

---

[13] At the same time, sometimes.

other, and I raced myself every week to try to raise the bar on my previous lesson.[14]

A-level teaching

This presents unusual and exacting challenges to any teacher. The benefits are that the students are older, hopefully more mature, and more motivated due to the self-selected nature of the course (in other words, they don't have to be in your lesson, which provides you with a nice chip to play in behaviour management: pull up your socks, or do the long walk). The subject can be discussed at a level that you might find engaging. The students can also be usually trusted to participate in much more challenging and demanding activities and learning styles.

The drawbacks are that it requires a much more thorough level of proficiency from the teacher. The demands of A-level prohibit 'winging' it on any level; the students will see right through it. Also, given that the students occupy that strange Twilight Zone where they feel entitled to the privileges of adulthood but also the carefree irresponsibility of childhood (a state from which most will have barely left), they can be unusually awkward: this usually manifests itself in lateness, absenteeism and resistance to homework tasks that involve sustained effort.[15]

◆ Read far, far ahead in the syllabus. Aim to have read through everything that you need in order to teach them before the course starts. If you stay one or two pages ahead of them (which although inadvisable you can get away with in Year 7), then they will rumble you as a chancer, simply by asking you a question which exceeds your weedy knowledge base.

◆ Read farther; go back to your university work if you have to; brush up on current developments (not too essential in Philosophy or Medieval History, but much more relevant in applied sciences. Even then, you should be aware of current events that could be used as conceptual examples in your classes. Popular culture is handy to know too, so that you can make comparisons between it and whatever you are teaching as a useful point of reference).

---

[14] I still use some of the resources from those days, untouched by subsequent experience. And believe me, I can't say that about much I did then.

[15] It's long, man. Funny how some teenagers sound like old hippies.

♦ Be completely aware of the scheme of work; you need to know where the lessons are going at a detailed *and* a global level. Get everything in context.

♦ Be completely aware of the marking scheme, and get the students practising it as soon as possible. If you need practice marking the essays, then get as much as possible, and as early on as possible. And that means they'll certainly need the experience too. One great activity for them to do is to mark each other's papers, based on the mark scheme, which you will have clearly explained to them in the first place. You can then mark it after them, and essentially mark their marking. OfSTED will actually fall in love with you if you do things like that.[16]

Bitches, snitches, zombies: low level disruption

Broadly speaking, the best advice for the new teacher to get the kids behaving is to be fair, to have rules, to be consistent and to do what you say, every time. You need to be the cliff that they dash themselves against until they give up through exhaustion and submit to your mighty will; and if your will doesn't feel so mighty, then don't show it. The class really doesn't care about your fraying nerves, the pressure you're under, the stress and the hard work you put in. Honestly, they don't. If you try to get sympathy from them they will start secretly filming you in the hope that you'll do something they can put on YouTube. And if you start to rant at them about how much work you do for them only to be met with indifference, they will telepathically murmur 'But you're paid to do this,' and they'll be right.

That structure of control needs to be the framework within which you operate; the kids will see you mean business and are prepared to go the distance. But that's the longer strategy, and you will need to be able to handle specific behaviour as it arises, and arise it will. Even as you proceed along the path of resolute stubbornness, you may experience so many mini-revolts and coups d'état you will suspect that your classroom is in fact Nigeria.[17]

The simple solution is to treat long-term, low-key disruption as a cumulative event, and if several small events happen successively,

---

[16] Which may not encourage you. Sometimes good ideas and OfSTED coincide. Presumably unintentionally.

[17] *Loves* a good coup. Has them instead of elections.

then you simply redefine that as equivalent to a larger, more disruptive event. Or in other words, if it gets up your nose, get them in trouble. Keep them in at the end and apply sanctions as you see fit. If they huff and puff, and complain that they didn't really do anything and you're so unfair, calmly remind them that anything anyone does in the room to impede learning will feel the naughty sword; and right now, that means them.

Sometimes pupils like that have issues with authority, and they're working it out with someone whom they perceive to be a vulnerable, weaker extension of the school authority. Sometimes they need to be reminded who's boss; sometimes they are expressing adolescent anxiety, and are trying to recompense low self-esteem by basking in the glow of peer approval.

On the other hand, who cares? They can bloody well behave in your classroom. You have a duty to teach the class, and if a child wants to chain herself to the desk and try to derail your engine of education, bulldoze over them. That'll teach them.[18]

The second placement was much more about doing the job, and much less about reflection. There were no observations after the first week (I spent nine weeks there in total as the weather turned brighter, the days got lighter, and life seemed easier) apart from a couple of official ones, so the main feedback I got was from my students, who were happy to let me know when things were going wrong.

'This is boring,' one would say. Out came my paltry naughty stick.

'Don't be cheeky. What's your name?' I said.

'Jim,' he replied.

'Jim what?'

'Jim Beam, sir.' My pencil lead broke.

'What did I say about cheek?' I said, not having it for one minute. The boy rolled his eyes. Another pupil spoke:

'It is too his name, sir. Check the register.' I did. There it was; Jim Beam. Some parents are sadists. Come back, Queenelizabeth.

---

[18] There is an element of frivolity in my metaphor. I do care about why they misbehave, I really do; it helps me understand how to deal with them. But if you're teaching twenty-five children, twenty-five lessons a week or there-abouts, you don't have time to give them a hug and cry about how nobody understands them. Sorry, but you just can't. You have too much to do. Maybe that's sad, but until we get the time and the training to do so, you're a teacher, first and foremost, and their personal issues will have to take a ticket and get in line.

Waiting for silence

Opinion is divided on this one. Some say you should wait for as long as it takes, and I have sympathy for this view. In my opinion, unless the class is fairly feral, they will at least allow you to speak at first, before deciding how to react to you, so in almost every circumstance you should make it clear that you will not begin until you have their complete attention, facing front, mouths shut. It sends out a powerful signal to the kids: what I have to say is important, and I won't stand for any nonsense. However, with some classes there will be one or two, or even a small group who blatantly ignore you in order to make your life Hell. Stay calm. Memorize their faces, find out their names by the end of the lesson, and then introduce them to a world of sanction pain. Teach them the error of their ways. If you do get one of those classes where silence is never achieved, and they're plainly mugging you off, you might have to proceed to the next step, which is setting some work – perhaps a simple board task or book activity. While the silent students are doing this, you can get to work on the awkward squad; more on this later.

Assuming that you have waited for a while with an utterly impassive look on your face, you should be looking at a reasonably silent class. Then you can begin. If you just begin without trying to

WHAT'S THE POINT OF ENGLISH? WE'LL NEVER USE IT!'

LITERACY

get them silent, you tacitly allow them to think that you can be talked over. That's a dangerous lesson to teach them.

In my first encounters with a new class, I spend the best part of thirty to forty-five minutes talking to them about the rules and expectations of the classroom. I don't recommend this tactic for everyone, because I'm very comfortable talking at a class for extended periods. But set your stall out from the start; communicate your behaviour rules to them, either in written form to be stuck in their books, or verbally, or by writing them on the board, or by conveying it in the form of a mime[19] – anything that gets it in their heads. The fact that you start talking about it first shows how important it is to you. Of course in the first lesson you will have other things to do – you might give an overview of the curriculum, or why your subject is important. But believe this: behaviour in your lessons is absolutely axiomatic to good learning; if they won't behave, then their learning will happen despite your best efforts, not because of them. So start on behaviour, and then you can introduce your bloody fifteen-part lessons later.

As the placement drew to a close, I checked my Professional Development Portfolio, my college Bible of progress, and realized that there were several key areas that I had still barely prodded with my educational probe: mainly something called 'Teaching and Learning'. This seemed to apply to everything we were doing in schools, so I didn't know how to understand the term as something separate from every other activity. It was a bit like being a fish and being asked to investigate 'being wet'.

It got worse; I realized I had covered a fraction of the topics: the 14–19 curriculum; EAL[20] pupils (that was easy; I could confidently say that the strategy to deal with them was to hand out colouring in pictures. Next?); Citizenship and something called PSHE, which a kind teaching assistant told me was Personal, Social and Health Education, or condoms, voting and wiping your ass.[21] 'Feedback to other parents' was the next gripping topic, 'Key Stage Transitions', which is so unspeakably uninteresting that I can hardly bring myself to type it, and of course, equal opportunities, which was I suppose inevitable.

What surprised me was how formal and institutionalized everything was in teaching, at least in theory. All the topics I have just mentioned were

---

[19] Don't, for God's sake.

[20] English as an Additional Language.

[21] Years later, that still describes it perfectly adequately. You will probably have to teach some of this when you get a real job, because Satan runs the world, apparently.

spoken of in serious tones, and were obviously very grave topics whenever our training was being discussed. In the classroom, on the other hand, they were footnotes to the actual experience of being a teacher, which isn't to say that equal opps and so on aren't important, but let me assure you they are the last thing on your mind when you are struggling up the coalface of becoming a professional teacher. My thoughts were far more preoccupied with remembering names, working out how to turn an overhead projector on, learning about the life of Muhammad so that I could teach it the next day, and trying to ignore the pupils when they obviously addressed me as 'the vegetable.'

Back at the Institute we were being lectured to about racism and teaching refugees, the Tomlinson report (later ignored by the incumbent Ministry for Education, or Mini-Ed for short) and inclusion again. We even had a meeting with an expert on inclusion issues at the second placement, and we were expected to visit a beacon school for inclusion, but I developed a tickly throat that day. Boy, they sure did think inclusion was important. I was too busy looking for an enquiry to find evidence for. And a pen that worked.

Something you must remember is that you are not a social worker or a child psychologist. You aren't a police officer or a nurse. You are a teacher, and you can only do so much for the people in your care. If you have done your best for all of them, then you should go home and sleep easy at night. You will never 'cure' or 'fix' the people you look after, because you can't. Don't take their problems home with you, or stew over the injustices of the world, because your shoulders aren't broad enough for that kind of tragedy and pain. Just fix the things in front of you that you can, and move on. That's all any of us can do with the powers we have. This is good advice in life generally, but never more so than when working in the public sector, where you will see more than your fair share of misery, helplessness, sadness and waste. Teach. Teach to the best of your ability, and look after the ones you look after. Make your job meaningful, but remember it is a job; something that you do as part of your life. If you open your arms to save them all, you will break with disappointment.

The upside of this somewhat sad outlook is that you can do a lot with the ones you have; you can help them; you can perhaps inspire them. You can show them different ways of thinking and living, and loosen the mental shackles they have lived with since birth. And then you move on and try with the next lot. That's your gift and your responsibility.

Worryingly, some of my peers had been offered jobs at their placement schools. I think I gave off an entirely false sense of bravado, so my nonchalance at not even having started yet was viewed by some of my more anxious colleagues as reassuring, when in fact they should have ignored my studied indifference and started panicking. I certainly felt nothing; the future was an undiscovered country to me, and I trusted that fate would bring me to a safe shore.

The placement came to an end with greater regret than the first; we celebrated with sparkling wine in the garden and promised to stay friends forever, like in the Railway Children. Then we went to the pub and got smashed

STAKEHOLDERS.

PARENTS EVENING

'HOW IS MY SON EXPECTED TO DO HIS PROJECT
IF YOU WON'T LET HIM CUT AND PASTE FROM THE
INTERNET?'

There was a sense of unreality now; many of my friends had jobs lined up, and told stories about tutors who were awed and delighted by their aptitude and diligence; some of them had been recommended by their schools to other schools, where I imagined the students ran arm-in-arm across endless fields, laughing with their teachers and dreaming about the beautiful futures they were going to build, inspired by the kind, wise and supportive colleagues who had got jobs when I hadn't. The b*****ds. It was starting to bite now. For those of us, the left-behind, college was a different experience. We scoured the Times Educational Supplement, Britain's premier source of jobs pedagogic across the UK. The diversity of jobs on offer was baffling.

The lectures became more and more career-focused: applying for jobs; the Induction process and how to make it work for you; surviving the NQT year, and so on. Attendance was brisk, apart from the ones who knew where they would be going in September. Even more highly prized were the schools that offered a few weeks induction work before they broke up for the summer. That meant you were employed by the school before the holidays started, and given that teachers are salaried and not paid by piece, this was a pot of gold for the long break.

There were so many schools to investigate, let alone apply for. Our lecturer said that we had to consider the 'type' of school we wanted to be in, and narrow it down that way. But what did that mean? I had close experience of two polar opposites under my scrawny belt, and nodding acquaintance with two others, and one of them was my childhood alma mater. Faith school or non? Independent or state? Inner city, suburban or rural? Single-sex or co-educational? And those were just the obvious lines of demarcation: there were others, more subtle. School with a sixth form or not? Academy, comprehensive, grant-maintained, special school, further education college? Carousel teaching or discrete subjects? Democratic, progressive managerial style, or autocratic and strict?

My second placement had shown me that I would be a nervous wreck if I started my career in a tough school. A kind colleague pointed out a vacancy in the East End; a Church of England school with a long lineage. A visit to the area showed that it had the variegation so ubiquitous to East London: faded but grand Victorian housing, civic buildings and sprawling parks, Siamese-stitched on to sixties prefabricated social housing side-by-side. It wasn't without charm: it was urban and very, very alive. It was exactly the kind of thing that London is good at; manic, mixed vibrancy. There were rough spots and smooth – the school was on a leafy avenue of the latter. My application went in, like a message in a bottle, and I waited.

At college I handed in my Evidence Based Enquiry; it was marked and returned, with feedback – it was acceptable, rather than exceptional, as I knew it was. Even an Arts graduate recognizes that a few nights in the Education faculty library and a day of redrafting doesn't guarantee premium academic results. Some might even say it would impede the quality of the final product.[1] The academic year ended with a whimper; we celebrated with snacks in the tutorial room (although of course, because we were an RS group, everyone brought matzo, halal kebabs and oddly, sushi.[2] Nobody knew whether to bless it or sacrifice it. So we scoffed it, religiously). Like

---

[1] I pour scorn on such reactionary philosophies.
[2] Well, it's efnic, innit?

school, the end trickled away without ceremony so we all hugged goodbye in ethnically specific ways – very little high-fiving and chest bumping, I'd like to point out.

I still had no job. And then one of my applications came back with an interview offer.

Applying for jobs

I have looked at thousands of application forms in my time. A job might receive dozens of applicants; several are selected, and like *Highlander*, there can be only one at the end. It's a Darwinian survival of the fittest.

The raison d'être of the application form is to weed out the unsuitable. By a bit of logical jiggery pokery we can conclude that the key thing your application form must do is commit no mistakes. Sure, you need to stand out a little and it helps if you look like the ideal candidate on paper, but that's not the function of the form. Remember the function is to eliminate you. So don't give the employer any reason to think that you're not suitable. It's an inversion of the Tall Poppy syndrome. Don't look obviously awful. Such things will include:

◆ Poor spelling. For God's sake, spell check the thing. And then *read* it, because spell checks don't correct every stylistic tick and idiosyncrasy of their human operators. If you type something sufficiently random the computer just goes, 'Ah, the master must know what he's doing,' and ignores it. Poor spelling just gives the impression that you are sloppy, stupid or don't care.

◆ Unexplained gaps in your career. Sure, you might have been climbing the Eiger, building an orphanage in Namibia or taking a maternity break, but unless you spell it out, your employers will think you did time in Barlinnie, or just enjoy signing on. Don't give the impression that you're hiding anything.

◆ Irrelevant detail. You may have won the school art prize three years running, but unless you can make an explicit link between that and the role you're applying for, it will seem like chaff; worse, it will look like a generic CV you send to any job. Tailor it to teaching, and prioritize experience, skills and history that show you can teach, work with children and know your subject area.

◆ A covering letter full of unsubstantiated character claims. So you're 'innovative, creative and enthusiastic'? Why should they believe you? Anyone can boast – give examples of when you have demonstrated these traits in the last year or so, and your claims will look much more secure. And avoid cliché: if I read another letter where the applicant claims to be 'good with people' and a 'self-starter', I'll invite them in just so I can chin them.

◆ A picture. Are you mental?

On my big day I wore my least cheap suit and my lucky pants.[3] The process seemed to be a standard one: a tour, then a demonstration lesson, then an interview. I was sweating as I had never done for an interview in my life. It wasn't just the lateness in the year; I also wanted to do well. I had stumbled and clowned through my PGCE year, but in the end I had passed; I even had a certificate to guarantee this. Sometimes I looked at it just to remind myself.

Early; I arrived early, of course. So early I paced up and down in front of the school smoking cigarettes to kill time. Once inside I was introduced to a member of the senior staff, the Head of Humanities, and the Head of Department, which was a lot of information and names at once for my liking; too many names and something has to fall out to make space.[4]

The application form indicated that there were IT facilities. I wanted to do a jazzy PowerPoint to show them how groovy and computer-literate I was, so I had already phoned up and checked.

'Hi,' I said, 'I'm interviewing for a post tomorrow. Can I just confirm that there will be IT facilities in the room I'm teaching in?' The person at the other end answered without a second's pause:

'Of course there will be!' she said breezily.

I walked into my demonstration classroom. There were, of course, no IT facilities, unless they were disguised as an abused whiteboard and a TV that hung from the ceiling like a dystopian disco ball. My inquisitors (two of them) sat smiling at the back, and the class were looking at me for the authority that started to seep away through my toes into the floor. But with ingenuity borne of an entire career dealing with cock-ups, I had had the foresight to print off a room full of hard copies of my slides, so I breezily went from hi-tech to old-school without missing a beat.

---

[3] I'm lying, of course: all my suits are cheap.

[4] Someone once said that the trick was to look them in the eyes when you're being introduced, hold the gaze and then repeat their name, slowly. Don't do this. You will look like a mentalist.

The school website cheerily suggested that 'We like our lessons to engage our students visually, aurally, and kinaesthetically!'[5] Catchy.[6]

So I got them all to stand up. With the constant amazement of the new teacher, I nearly fainted when they did so; it's exhilarating when people do as you ask them to with no disagreement. It seemed the kids here, though a bit rough round the edges, would be more amenable to the joys of education. I did a bit of standard teacher jiggery-pokery with them; got them to sit down for various reasons and demonstrated social isolation by leaving one sad soul standing for a minute while I carried on teaching ('So how did you feel standing there by yourself? Ah, lonely and weird. That's excellent – why don't we give him a big clap!' That sort of thing). Then it was reading, pair work, a group survey, finished off with individual work in their books (on the paper I brought in case they decided to nutmeg me with 'no equipment'). I'm not saying it was brilliant, but I could hear the boxes being ticked at the back of the room. I crammed about ten activities into twenty minutes, and it felt like I'd scaled the Eiger wearing baseball gloves.

Teaching a sample lesson

Most schools will ask you to teach a lesson, or part of a lesson, on the day of the interview. You will have been informed about this when you get the call back after a successful application letter, including information about the age group and the subject to teach. Do check in advance about the availability of IT before you get there, although given my experience perhaps it wouldn't hurt to ask for a second opinion.[7] Make clear how long you have to teach. On the one hand you have the advantage that the children will be unsure about you, and will hopefully give you the behavioural benefit of the doubt at least as long as it takes for you to get in there, teach and scarper. Plus the observers sitting at the back of the lesson will have a pacifying effect on the class for a short while, although it can wear off quickly. Try to ignore them.

---

[5] VAK learning styles were all the rage back then they still are in some schools. The jury is very out on whether such things exist in a meaningful way, so I wouldn't panic if your classes don't learn Physics through the medium of ballet, or whatever.

[6] I liked the jaunty exclamation mark, indicating what? Geniality? Surprise? Shouting?

[7] I kid, I kid. Saying, 'Are you sure?' to the person on the phone will look cheekier than two Cheeky Girls.

♦ Make sure you write a lesson plan for the observers. Stick to it, unless it looks like you have to change mid-flow to cater for something unexpected. And make it a detailed plan to explain the reasoning for everything you do, in case it's not obvious.

♦ Keep the pace brisk with several activities.

♦ Vary the style of the activities to generate interest from different sections of the class.

♦ Build in some automatic differentiation/challenge.

♦ Be stern and assertive, but for God's sake don't get angry or nasty in your observation lesson (indeed, ever) because the kids will look at each other, then at you and telepathically decide to boycott your lesson.

♦ Have a back up – bring in hand-outs, or an extra activity in case you run out of things for them to do (God, the Horror, the Horror).

Then the interview. Four bodies in a grand old Head's office and me, sat in a circle, which I thought was very egalitarian. We shook hands and I left feeling that if I didn't get the job, then it was because the other candidates were better, because I gave it the lot. I guess in the end that's all you can do. Everything else is just worrying after nothing.[8]

I got it; I celebrated with a bottle of wine that was worth less than the Happy Meal it washed down. I was nearly at the stage of selling my hair to the children of Russian diplomats to pay the rent, so getting the call meant a Hell of a lot more than it might have done to someone else. And it started before summer ...

The interview

If you've got to the interview stage it means that you could possibly do the job. It means that as far as your prospective employers are concerned, you might be the Golden Child. Don't you feel better already?

---

[8] If you get one of those mentalist interviews you hear about where the employer is wearing a cowboy hat, sitting on top of the cupboard and asks you to do a cartwheel, then walk out immediately, setting off the fire alarm as you do so. Anything more outré than 'Tell me a joke' and they can stick their job up their backside, frankly.

Be prepared

Oh, if only the unifying maxim of the International Boy Scout Movement were adopted as a universal creed among all men. There is an enormous amount you can do before the interview that will get you light years ahead; in fact, the preparation you do will be like the enormous, submarine part of the iceberg, and the interview is the tip. First of all, scrutinize the school's website in depth. You are serious about getting this job, right? Then spend a while looking at what the school is trying to say to the world. This is their shop window, and if you look unsure about what type of school it is, what the ethos is or some of the history underlying it, then you'll look totally unprofessional. So get to know it, and focus on the history, the school vision, the curriculum and any major projects and achievements that the school seems proud of. It certainly doesn't hurt either to familiarize yourself with some of the key names. You should also explore other sources of information about the school. If you're feeling keen, visit the school prior to the interview and check out the area, the feel of the school and how the kids react to you before you (hopefully) start work there.

Second, find out who will be interviewing you if this information is available and Google them. Find out their backgrounds, their interests, what kinds of projects they've been involved in. If you're really Machiavellian you can tailor your responses to appeal to their interests, although this might be pushing into the realms of creepy.

Third, be ready for the range of standard questions you will probably be asked. There is a potentially infinite number they can hit you with, but they'll probably land in a predictable range:

◆ Why are you a good candidate for this role?
◆ How are you?[9]
◆ Why do you want to be a teacher?
◆ Why do you want to be a teacher here?
◆ What are your weaknesses?[10]
◆ Tell us about yourself.[11]

---

[9] I don't often give answers for you, but I'll give you a clue: 'Fine, thanks' is what they're grasping for.

[10] Resist the temptation to say 'Kryptonite' or 'women'. Funny, but deal-breakers. So is, 'You.'

[11] That one's a belter. Some people freeze for so long you can nip out and have a fag, and they're still thinking.

- What would you do if a student refused to do what you asked them to?
- What do you know about the school?
- What are your strengths?
- How do you deal with pressure?
- What's your favourite book/movie, etc?

Be pleasant; be polite. Smile, and make eye contact. You'd think these were obvious, but I've seen people fail to do all three time and time again. Look pleased to be there, and not too intimidated, otherwise you'll look like a pushover. I recommend a firm handshake across the table with everyone who'll be speaking to you. Men: don't look a complete tosser by wringing the hand of the headmaster. If they offer you water, accept it: your throat will dry out like a clay oven over the interview (which if it has any professional rigour should be over half an hour).

Dress to impress, of course. Senior staff tend to be very old school in their couture and you should too. You may dress like Frank 'n' Furter at the weekends, or take Rockabilly dance classes every night. My advice in this context is: if you expect to wear your piercings or Mohican in your daily job, then do so at the interview, and let your potential employers assess it there and then. If you cover up something that you consider to be stylistically important then you should be honest and display it at interview. But if you take out all the lip studs for the interview and then turn up on day one looking like Pinhead, then your employer has a right to complain.

You will probably have to speak to a panel; make sure that you speak to all of them. Direct your answers principally at the person who questioned you, but make sure that you make eye contact with everyone else at least once in your answers. Your answers should be much longer than the questions; if they ask you a short question, then talk for a few minutes, perhaps longer if you want to expand upon your answers, but certainly five to ten minutes maximum. You want to appear confident and knowledgeable without sounding nervously pedantic.

Turn up early, incidentally. And don't swear.[12]

---

[12] Obvious, I know, but I once interviewed candidates for a management position where the hopeful kept saying, 'Christing,' repeatedly, which apart from being inappropriate, was also one of the oddest swear words I'd ever heard.

Day one was two weeks after the interview. Interestingly I had been hired with another teacher for the same department, and the Head of the Department had also been replaced, so we were a relatively young and very new team. The next three weeks until the end of term were to be engaged in induction, taking the first Bambi-steps towards fitting into school.

The pre-induction

If you are terrifically fortunate, you may be able to land a job that starts immediately prior to the summer break which has the benefit of paying your rent/mortgage for a few months and also allows you to enjoy the benefit of a pre-induction period. This is gold dust; you have been given a safe zone to watch the school, learn how it thinks, and where you fit into it. You get to introduce yourself to some of the classes you'll be teaching, and your timetable will *never* be as light again. Savour it: these are the glory weeks.

This should be a compulsory feature of teacher induction.[13] If you get a job that starts in September, or worse, one that starts later in the year, then you will have to hit the ground running; the kids, the timetable and the school won't give you any space to breathe when you get started. As far as the kids are concerned you're a teacher, simple as that, and they will expect you to act like one. They might give you a honeymoon period of behaviour because they're glad to back at school (believe it or not, they do get bored in the long holidays) and they're not sure if you're going to rip their heads off. Once they've established that you're not then it's open day. That's all you get from them.

Normally, pre-induction weeks will take place in the last few weeks of the Summer Term; the weather is getting sunnier, the teachers are knackered, and people's thoughts turn, not to love, but to wrapping things up. The kids agree, and the heat, humidity and imminent freedom combine to create a sense of restlessness in the classrooms. Into this peculiar blend of lethargy and enthusiasm you step. You will be expected to take on a light timetable, although for you it will feel like you have been clobbered with the twelve tasks of

---

[13] Or at least, before the banking system decided to play Monopoly with your granny's pension funds and the leaders of the Western World had to check behind everyone's sofas for spare change to pay the same bankers to keep lending us money. Or something; I don't teach economics, I might be a little off.

Hercules – even one or two lessons a day can feel an enormous task to the new teacher; this is mainly down to the enormous amount of conscious planning you will put into it. Uncertainty breeds in every teacher a desire to plan, plan, plan, and until you teach the lesson, it will occupy your thoughts constantly. Of course.

The staff room was a barometer of the school corpus. This one was old-fashioned, needed a lick of paint, but friendly and social; the last one had felt like Robocop's knickers. Of course, no matter how sociable a school is, you'll always be the new one. I made what was apparently the obvious opening gambit – walking up to people and introducing myself, making a minute's small talk and then buzzing off respectfully. Obviously, I didn't shoehorn myself into any conversations, or approach anyone actively crying or playing the spoons.

Beware; you are still the rookie. In most social environments, territories are well marked, scents invisibly dispensed by the Lords of the Jungle; it took me a few days/weeks to realize where new staff were meant to sit, and what were considered to be acceptable activities for them to do. Hint: sitting with your fellow new teachers and loudly marvelling how few periods you had to teach, and wasn't it all fabulous? is not one of those things. I also discovered the value of having a mug. Even my Nan's Nan knows that teachers drink more tea than the P.G. tips monkeys, and so it proved. We had the luxury of free caffeine, probably in much the same way that Vietnam soldiers were tacitly free to smoke pot and get smashed while off duty, on the quiet understanding that it was a cheap safety valve against them going postal with a million dollar's worth of ordnance.

Using someone's favourite, favoured mug was a huge faux pas; one charmer came up to me as I was mid-sip and said, 'Are you finished with my cup yet?' The label indicating ownership was, alas, invisible. She actually stood and waited for me to finish, so I went to the sink, poured it out, and handed it back, still warm and guilty from my illicit beverage exploitation. Thank God the police weren't involved. I bought my own the next day. It said, 'Nearly a teacher!!!' with a picture of a cross-eyed rabbit wearing a corduroy jacket. I imagined no one would want to steal it, and I was right.

Upon your entrance to the pre-induction, you will have a series of meetings from people welcoming you to the school: a member of the Senior Leadership Team[14] responsible for new members of staff; your

---

[14] This used to known as the Senior Management Team, but the concept of management didn't sound dynamic enough, so now everyone wants to be a leader, apparently. I used to stack shelves in a supermarket; I was described as a 'Par manager.' I fuss you not.

Head of Department; perhaps the Head of Year (or Head of Learning as the role is mostly called now[15]) you could be assigned to; maybe a mentor, either a professional one or a pastoral one (also called a 'buddy'[16]) to name but a few. These are the ones you should shake hands with firmly and look in the eye as you repeat their names (despite my earlier warnings) because they can be immensely helpful if they want to, and if you let them. If they suggest a meeting, agree. If they don't, then you should suggest one. Don't hide yourself away, because this is the best time in the year to get to know people, to learn the layout of the school, the hierarchy of management, who you need to know and who you can get to know if you like; where the tea bags are; which kids need which strategies, where the bus stop is and where the toilets are. It won't be this easy for long, so make the most of it. And although it's pointless of me to say it: try to relax. This is a fantastic job. If it wasn't so hard, it wouldn't be so rewarding. Get stuck in.

---

[15] 'Head of Year' also wasn't sexy enough.
[16] Sorry, but when I hear 'Buddy' I think of someone working in Dunkin' Donuts who isn't allowed to use the machines.

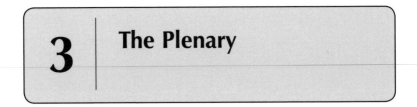

'GRATEFUL AS WE ARE FOR THE PAGES OF 'WAYS FORWARD' CAN YOU TELL US WHAT WE GOT, SO WE CAN ESTABLISH OUR TRADITIONAL PECKING ORDER OF HUMILIATION?'

EMPATHY.

HOMEWORK:

'OF COURSE I FEEL YOUR PAIN. RIGHT NOW, IT'S IN MY ASS.'

Preparing over summer

After your pre-induction (if you had one) you face the prospect of six lovely weeks before you start the job properly. It goes without saying (so I'll say it) that you should pick up a copy of the schemes of work, syllabuses and any resources the department has to help you teach your first term. In terms of planning, it's fair to say that you should have planned your first two weeks worth of lessons down to the resources and differentiation before you start. It will seem onerous, but the more you can do in Summer to get ready for your first week the better. The first weeks are overwhelming, and more so if you have to plan all your lessons too; instead, get that part of the job out of the way, and then you can focus on delivering the lessons, behaviour and other matters of orientation.

- Pick up syllabuses and schemes of work. Read the bloody things.
- Get used to the layout of the school, and where all the important rooms are – toilets, staffroom, your classrooms, the office, the head's office, the department rooms and offices, the playground (!), the canteen, the sin bin. Don't be 'the teacher wandering around looking lost'. Some schools have maps, so ask for one.
- Draw up seating plans and get class lists so that you can notionally have them seated and organized before they enter the room.
- Brush up on any topic you'll be teaching if it feels rusty to you.

The danger in this period is that you will over-plan. Depending on how tense you feel, you may be obsessing about it all a bit, or constantly worrying that there is something else you should be doing to get 'readier'. There probably isn't, unless you're being really slack. Get your lessons planned, get your bearings, and that's most of what you need to do. Teaching is an activity where you are learning all the time, and a considerable amount of it is done on the hoof; you can only plan so much before you're simply planning to relieve anxiety. So don't kill yourself; enjoy your Summer Break (if you have one) and get rested. You'll need it.

Those first weeks were some of the strangest I have ever experienced in my professional life; in at the deep end doesn't describe it. Despite all the benefits of the pre-induction, the actual beginning to the induction year is a shock to the system comparable to the scalding hot/freezing cold Turkish bath cure. Let me describe how I felt in one word: busy. I had worked in Soho bars and restaurants on Saturday nights, New Years Eves, bank holidays and Notting Hill Carnivals; I have never felt a keener sense of relentless, endless labour and disorganization as I did in those weeks.

Starting out

Your first day will probably be strangely child-free; that's because most schools have an INSET day (which stands for In Service Training; someone worked hard to make that into a word) where the school will offer a combination of training sessions, staff meetings, Head Teacher's reports and department planning time. The purpose of the day is for staff to get ready for the challenges of the new year, be briefed about important school plans, and prepare resources and facilities for the imminent intake.

It also serves an enormous social purpose as colleagues and friends re-establish links, swap stories and compare tans/shark bites. This is just as important. As a new member of staff you might feel a little bit alienated from all of this jollity, or intimidated by the gears of the school machine starting to turn again after six rusty weeks. This is all normal, of course. Meet as many people as possible, and focus on the people you need to meet if you haven't done this already: various members of the hierarchy who can help you, and whom you need to work with. Get a relationship started with these people before you need to call on it, and you'll find that it becomes a lot easier to work alongside others. If you only speak to people when you need them, then you clearly signal that you're only interested in them for their utilitarian value.

Practical matters: pick up a planner. Most schools provide a teacher diary of some sort where you can keep all your useful information: class lists, lesson titles, extra-curricular duties you may have, meeting schedules, important calendar dates, names, notes and any other jottings you may have, all in one place. I usually find it useful to stick a copy of my timetable into it as well and a map if you can get your hands on one. This planner will become your best friend, so treat it like a pal; don't lose it, leave it or give it to a kid to carry. Treat it like your mobile phone or wallet; when you leave a classroom, pat yourself down to see if you know where it is. Increasingly it will become full of confidential details, phone numbers, detention notes etc., so give it some respect.

If you haven't already done so, draw up your seating plans, using a rough picture of where all the tables are in the classroom. Of course, you can design your own table layout if you want, although bear in mind the time it might take you to do this for every lesson, especially if you have to get the kids to do it for you. Also consider if you want to be moving everything back at the end of the lesson.

You should have a meeting with your new Head of Department, and if not, make one. You need to sit down with them and show them the lessons you've planned. They need to look at them closely and give you any last minute advice about suitability, ways forward and tips to improve them. There will undoubtedly be something you haven't thought of: maybe a set of textbooks is double booked for a lesson; maybe your computer research lesson will be in a broom cupboard – anything is possible.

Finally, make sure all your resources are ready for the next day. I cannot emphasize how important this is: many are the teachers who condemn themselves to lives of anxiety and stress by photocopying everything on the day or worse, ten minutes before the lesson starts. That kind of bungee jumping might get your adrenalin pumping, but who needs it? The photocopier might be jammed when you need it urgently, and then you're snookered. The books will be locked in a cupboard that no one has the key to. Or the coloured paper has run out. Or ... there are just too many variables. Keep them to a manageable minimum by getting your gear together the day before, and go home and sleep easy.

Well, as easily as possible.

First contact

This where you start to put everything you have learned into practice; this is where the practice becomes practice. Hopefully you got a good night's sleep and a hearty breakfast, because you'll need to be in good shape for the challenges ahead of you. You're dressed smart and comfortably; your resources are all trimmed and copied, and your planner is tidy and mostly empty. Time, Mr Pink, to go to work. I feel nervous just writing it. You probably will too. This is perfectly normal.

I've briefly mentioned the mental state of the teacher in the section on Status; this is something worth mentioning briefly again. You may well be absolutely wracked with nerves on your first day. Some people experience feelings of self-doubt so complete that they feel as though they're going to turn inside out. The worst thing about feeling insecure is that you imagine everyone else shares your opinion of yourself, and that it is obvious to anyone that looks at you, like a paranoid stoner.

Get in nice and early – this is not the day to be rushing in at the last minute. Have all your resources ready to hand, and make sure you know exactly where all of your classrooms will be. Check if the rooms are locked and need a key to access, otherwise you'll be looking for cracks in the floor to swallow you up when you get locked out with the rest of the class. If you have free time before the lesson starts, be there ten minutes early and set the room up; tidy it, arrange the chairs and desks as you wish. You might like to put an exercise book on every desk, along with the requisite textbook/sheet/other resource that the students will need. It gives off a huge sign that you are organized, ready, and care about their education.

Finally, stand by the door and when the bell goes off, stand in the doorway, visible to corridor and classroom alike, greeting them as they come in. Direct them to the back of the room ... and you're off. Good luck to you.

First of all, my timetable seemed impossible to meet. In my placements I had been expected to teach eight, then 12 lessons a week, which seemed nearly impossible. Here I was expected to wrestle with twenty five lessons, which on a thirty lesson week, left me with five fabulous non-contact lessons.[1] Although as a teacher on my NQT year I was entitled to a 10 per cent reduction in timetable, I had been told that this would not be possible. The nominal reason given was that I had been recruited as a FastTrack teacher, which meant that I would be expected to work to a higher level than other trainee teachers. It didn't exactly tickle me, but I did what most new recruits would have done in my position, and rolled over; twenty-five it was.

One of the reasons I'd wanted the job here was because, as a Church of England School, Religious Studies was given a relatively high status in the curriculum; two lessons a week for the young 'uns, and a compulsory GCSE for every one. And it had an A-level, which is where I wanted to go. So unlike some schools where it was relegated to an embarrassing cough on a carousel of humanities subjects (because, you know, they're all the same thing, aren't they?[2]), it took top billing with other non-core subjects (who are, as it were, the A-listers of the curriculum). The downside of such a prominent subject was that it meant, between myself and the other two RS teachers, we saw just under a thousand kids in a week. For the mathematically gifted that broke up into about three hundred kids apiece; three hundred names to learn. I could see that personalized learning was going to be a bit of an uphill struggle.

The INSET day was jolly enough, as I and the other trainees sat with our departments like pets and felt special. Most of the day I spent shuttling between mentors and the Head of Department. An awful lot of people asked me if I was OK, which was sweet for a while, until I started to feel vaguely bereaved. My Head of Department, Judith, had just been promoted to the post, and had only been in teaching for a few years; but just as a child always imagines anyone over fifteen is an adult, she seemed enormously competent and professional to me. Fortunately, she was.

---

[1] Which made it sound like the other 25 I was Thai boxing with them.

[2] No.

Reinventing the wheel

When you start school one of the most terrifying prospects (after 'will it hurt?') must be 'how on earth do I teach this lesson? As with your placement schools, the question of planning an endless stream of lessons seems like a hopeless task, and the feeling will multiply when you get a nearly full timetable. Unless your school has been created ex nihilo from the brow of Zeus, there will be resources already waiting to be used, so make life as easy for yourself as possible and see if anything the department has can be used. There should certainly be a scheme of work, some kind of description of what content and skills have to be covered on a term by term basis. The better planned the department, the more closely the scheme will be planned; some schools have individual lessons mapped out; some even have resources for each of the individual lessons. There will (or at least should be) appropriate textbooks/media for the courses you will teach, and you'd be a pretty odd fish if you didn't dip into them.

Note: 'until you get on your feet'. While it is famously inefficient to re-invent the wheel,[3] you also need to be developing lessons that are personal to you, your style, and the learning needs of your classes. It's no good aping the style of other teachers, or using lessons as if they were universal, because what works for one class may fall on stony ground with another. You'll never become the teacher you can be if you parrot someone else. Borrow, improvise and create. One day someone will be inspired by your lessons …

Teaching and learning: the aims of education

A huge topic, that goes right to the heart of education, because it invites us to ask, 'Why do we teach children? Or, 'What's the aim of education?' This is because it only makes sense to ask what the best way of doing something is if you have an idea of what it is you want to do. If you say that you want to get to Edinburgh, then it makes sense to ask, 'How should I get there?' In education, where is the 'there' you want to get to?

Luckily one or two people have thought about this question already. But it's a question that is almost entirely absent from every

---

[3] Has anyone actually ever done this? What on earth were they thinking? How did they feel when they got the bus home?

teacher training manual I have ever read; it's barely mentioned in the PGCE course, and steamboated over in favour of inclusion, differentiation and assessment for learning. One reason for this is that (and I don't wish to do a jig on a soapbox here) teacher training in state education is highly prescriptive. Education is run by and paid for by the state. It stands to reason that they might have a few aims in mind themselves in its construction and execution, and don't relish the idea of uppity teachers deciding what to do with all those classrooms and piles of funding. That's not reactionary griping, but perfectly understandable, if not desirable; I'm not sure I'd pour 30 per cent of my gross output into a sector and then say, 'Do your best, see what you can make of that lot then.'

The challenge for you as a teacher is to work out what the aims of education are nationally, the local aims, the school aims, the department aims ... and finally what your aims are. Shouldn't they all be the same? Not a bit of it. A wise man once said that education has no aims – education is a concept; only people have aims. People run education, deliver education, and because education isn't a concept that is settled equally in everyone's minds, there will always be disagreement about why we teach children.

Isn't it obvious why we teach? No. Consider the following candidates for the title of 'the aim of education.'

- to help children reach their potential
- to get them qualifications
- to train a workforce suitable for the national job market
- to compete internationally with other countries
- to create a harmonious society based on tolerance and respect
- to discover everyone's particular talents
- to provide basic life skills
- to provide a range of economically useful skills
- to prevent crime
- to monitor children while their parents work in the economy

I could go on. Many of these overlap, and some of them aren't mutually exclusive. But they are different, and many of them, if combined, exist in tension with each other. Can I teach someone to be a free spirit who listens to his heart, and also teach them to respect the law and figures of authority? Maybe, but I can see times when they might pull against each other. Should kids be allowed to learn what they want, and nurture their potential, or should they all be made to follow a national curriculum? Endless questions arise; answer them as you will. Rest assured that the aims of education have not been settled, nor perhaps ever will be. They are a question of values and opinions, and as such, you are as entitled to your perspective as anyone else.

Teaching and learning 2

So what are the best ways to teach students? And how do they best learn? The good news – which is also the bad news – is that after thousands of years of doing it, nobody really knows. Honestly. Despite what anyone tells you, education is not an exact science, and despite an enormous number of gurus, experts, researchers, government releases and INSETs, nobody can point conclusively to the best way of teaching or learning. If this sounds depressing, it shouldn't. Education is a social science; teaching is both an art and a craft. The way the mind learns is a matter not only for psychologists and neuroscientists, but also for philosophers. I cannot begin to tell you how many unknowns are involved in deciding these matters.

We barely understand how the brain works; we are only vaguely able to analyse what we even mean by consciousness and awareness. Psychology is one of the softest sciences there is, resting on assumptions that are untestable and unprovable – merely expedient. With all this uncertainty, is it any wonder that there is so much uncertainty about how to teach, and how to learn? Even extensive meta-studies of educational methods have failed to prove conclusively that one style of teaching is better than another. As William Goldberg famously said about Hollywood, 'No one knows anything.'

Almost. Just because we haven't been able to prove anything conclusively doesn't mean that we don't have some clues to guide us. Just because we aren't certain about what works doesn't mean we don't have any idea about what probably works. I am painfully alive to the fact that your first years in teaching are probably not the best time to be trawling through books of educational research, philosophy or theory (although you'll be battered with nuggets here and there to justify ideas that people will sell you, like Bloom's taxonomy, or Maslow's hierarchy of needs), so I'll summarize the basics for you:

Children seem to learn better when

- they are guided by an expert
- they actively investigate the subject
- they are encouraged to learn for themselves
- they find the subject interesting
- the learning area is safe and structured
- they learn in different ways

If you're disappointed how mundane these ideas are, then don't be. These are things that every teacher can achieve; there are no magic bullets in education, no amazing short cuts that only some teachers are doing. Pedagogy hasn't changed substantially in two thousand years, since Plato sent his students out to learn for themselves and report back to the class for a show and tell. Sure, the language has become more intricate, and the resources available reflect our cultures, but the paradigm hasn't changed: an expert leads a classroom of students, imparts knowledge and skills to them by a variety of methods, and tries to hold their interest. Along the way he ensures that the students are not sabotaging their own learning by failing to pay attention or disengage from the learning.

It's not rocket science, is it?

All state schools in England and Wales have to be inspected by OfSTED, which has a number of criteria for observation. The OfSTED reports, as mentioned, have an enormous influence on the school's status in the community, and most importantly on its desirability to parents as a place to send their children. Because schools now compete with each other for student numbers, this gives OfSTED an enormous clobbering device. As a result, the criteria as defined by OfSTED for a successful school have become the national paradigm and schools are desperate in almost every case to meet its criteria. Because they have an exacting definition of the aims of good teaching, you will be trained to meet these standards. As a member of a school, and as an emergent professional who wants to pass his/her induction year, it is essential that you understand and can demonstrate these standards. As a member of a profession with a duty to the welfare of children, it is also essential that you question those standards critically.

My line manager wanted to see two weeks of lesson plans in advance; I think I had about two days worth, and half of them were made up of 'getting to know you lessons', so for the first few weeks I tried to put it together, but never, I think successfully. As a result I felt like a perpetual failure. This was to be a common theme.

The first day was enormously busy; I taught every lesson without pause. But I seemed to be charmed, as a succession of six different classes went by; all of them complied with little difficulty to my requests and took the seating plans as suggested. With every single class I went through the same routine: handing out exercise books, handing out the class rules, handing out the syllabus, and then talking a bit about them. Inspired, eh? This is what's called being lulled into a false sense of security, the little rats. Day two I started to launch my lessons, and continued with the welcome lessons. Day three and four and things started to wobble. By the end of the week I had managed all my classes, but I was starting to wonder if I was beginning to lose them already. As Obi-Wan said, 'Trust your feelings, Luke,' because they were right.

Every night I went home and started to worry because I found it hard to prepare properly. The syllabus wasn't intelligible to me, and although I had the schemes of work and the internet links it just seemed too large, too global to translate into individual lessons. Even the resources that were available to me were old and plain, and I wanted to design lessons of my own that would interest and inspire them – and me. I didn't want to be the kind of teacher that turned up, did a job and left. I wanted to make learning fun, special and somehow transformative. Like most teachers, I didn't want to repeat the patterns of mistakes that teachers from my own youth had made. I wanted to be Robin Williams;[4] *Mr Chips; Scruffy McGuffy from Grange Hill.*

Inspirational teachers

Popular media are familiar with the tropes of the inspirational teacher, almost as much as it is with the cruel, perpetually dissatisfied teacher and the janitor with a secret. I think it's tremendously important for trainee teachers to enter the profession with a vision of the kind of teacher they want to become; I also think it's important to keep the vision flexible. John Keats from *Dead Poets* is not a real man, certainly not as portrayed, however ably, by Robin Williams. Plus he taught in a private school in the button-tight conservative fifties. If you imagine for one second that walking into a new class and asking them to shout their barbaric yawp across the rooftops of the world is the way a twenty-first century boy or girl learns, then you need a cold shower. Seriously; don't go in there imagining that you will, like

---

[4] In *Dead Poets' Society*, not *Patch Adams*, or *Insomnia*.

Miss Jean Brodie, grow a troop of devoted acolytes who will hang on your every word. Or, like Michelle Pfeiffer in *Dangerous Minds*, you'll pull a class of disaffected gang-bangers back from the brink of ghetto crime, into diplomas and college. It's all fiction; it happens, rarely, of course – these stories are often based on real stories – but they don't happen without context, and never like in the movies.

The reason why it's important to be realistic is that if you have enormous hopes for instant rapport and inspiration, you will be crushed by their indifference, and then possibly give up, your dreams in tatters. My aspiration is to keep your dreams alive by tying them to the real world. You can be the inspiration, but it's going to take time. In real life there is no montage to fast forward through the hard work you will have to do. Got that, Mr Chips?

Behaviour started to fall off a cliff, and I didn't know what to do. Some of the classes were responding reasonably well; some of the younger classes were easy to maintain, but even in some of them there were a few loudmouths, jokers and angry kids who clearly hadn't been told to treat respect for teacher as a priority. In those classes, even though most of the class behaved, it only took a few head bangers to ruin a lesson.

My reaction surprised even me; they frustrated me so much, so repeatedly, that I started to lose my temper. What kind of man was I, if I couldn't even keep a class of twelve-year-olds working quiet?

But the middle years, the infamous Year nines ... they started tearing me apart. I had three classes, and every one of them seemed to contain at least half a dozen kamikaze pilots, determined to explode in every lesson no matter what. It was all I could do even to get silence at the start of the lesson so I could give instructions. Most days I didn't, and just had to keep shouting as I explained what people had to do. There was no chance of getting the whole class doing something, or introducing the interesting activities I had planned; there simply wasn't a minute when somebody wasn't shouting out, or taking the mickey, or asking me personal questions.

I had no idea how to handle it. My style was listening to people, and having calm discussions; to me, reason was all, and I tried to tell the children that what they were doing was only hurting them. Then I started shouting at them that I had put a lot of effort into the lessons, and couldn't they see that? Then I just tried shouting at them. The Year nines just laughed. They stomped around the room and chatted constantly, left the room, called their friends and generally just did whatever they wanted for fifty minutes. When the bell rang I felt enormous relief, even if I was just shifting into another room of head bangers.

It didn't take long before it started getting to me. I sat late at school, staring at work I hadn't marked or lessons I needed to plan, and then went home and ignored all the work on my desk. I would plan lessons half-heartedly, pretending I didn't have to do them, and stare at work until I was too tired to stay awake any longer. But I felt like a total failure, because I had gone in with such high hopes: to entertain, inspire and lead them, only to find that they didn't give a snap.

That was the truth of it. Everything I tried to do was dashed against the wall of pupil indifference, and the distance between what they were capable of and what they wanted to do was heartbreaking. It was breaking my heart in other ways, and every night I sat and wept impotently as I planned, and dwelled on every failed lesson, every insult and every kid who laughed at me when I asked them to work.

What hurt most of all was that I genuinely cared about them. I wanted to help them and to share with them some of the things I found fascinating about other peoples' beliefs and philosophies. I'm painting a bleak picture because that's how it seemed to me. But the indifference of most of them was frightening. And the fact that some of them seemed to be downright nasty really got to me. They weren't as directly aggressive as the kids in my first placement, but as any teacher will tell you, it's often worse to be ignored or ridiculed than it is to have some thug half-heartedly tell you to f**k off. The latter takes a second, but the sting of the former stays with you a long, long time.

By December I had calcified into a pattern; half my classes behaved tolerably for me, and I could almost enjoy them. A quarter of my lessons I wanted to get through as quickly as possible, and the other quarter I dreaded. My peace of mind had gone the way of my self-esteem; I wasn't sleeping until two every morning, and I frequently woke up in the middle of the night worrying about some triviality. School, I must say, was making me feel quite wretched.

Your health

At the risk of sounding like your mother, the more you expect your body and mind to do, the more you'll need to look after it. I don't have to use a metaphor do I? If you were a car (you're not) and you expected to drive a thousand miles at a hundred miles an hour (this isn't a maths test), you'd probably take it in for a service first, and check the oil and petrol. Teacher training is an enormously difficult experience, and we often forget to look after the mechanisms that we need to keep going. If you're not going to go boogaloo, try the following:

1. get plenty of sleep, at regular intervals
2. eat healthily
3. get some exercise
4. take plenty of breaks
5. balance your work and play

Sounds completely bleeding obvious? You'd think so, wouldn't you? Many new teachers don't do any of these. Ask yourself which ones you're neglecting. You're not Superman.

So what was I doing about it? Nearly nothing. That's the shame of it; I was enduring it with what I felt was stoicism, but doing next to nothing to improve the situation. Looking back it seems impossible that I just sat and suffered it, but I didn't know what the alternatives were. My first two placements hadn't prepared me for dealing with these kinds of situation; I hadn't seen how these things were tackled, and I had never observed any teachers who knew what to do with this. I just assumed that I was cr*p; it's as simple as that. And when I joined the school, I remember being gravely told by an experienced member of staff that only weak teachers had problems with behaviour, or called for assistance. I didn't want to be a weak teacher.

I mostly stopped setting detentions, because when you told a kid that they had one, they just blew up in your face and caused an enormous scene, which guaranteed the rest of the class had a bit of a show for ten minutes.

What you're entitled to

When you start at school you will suffer from the same syndrome of any new recruit: you will be vulnerable, unsure of where you stand, and liable to the predations of the cruel and opportunistic. Which isn't to say that people will deliberately exploit you, at least not consciously but you will be more vulnerable now than at any other stage of your career. Many people will be happy to tell you what your role is. Some of them will have your best interests at heart; some of them will have other ideas, their own agendas to pursue. Their agenda might not be your agenda.

How might this manifest itself? The first thing to be careful of is that you receive your entitlement as a trainee teacher. This means:

◆ Protected time. You should not be teaching a full timetable;

currently the guideline is that you teach 90 per cent of a normal scheduled timetable.

◆ Induction training. The school is legally bound to provide you with training on a variety of on-going professional development skills and information points: teaching SEN, inclusion, behaviour management, and a host of others that change from year to year as DfE priorities change.

◆ An assigned mentor. This person is your lifeline; everyone at school is busy, and most are too busy to spare you the time you'll need. They are there to make time for you, and they will usually have volunteered for the position, so rejoice.

◆ Weekly progress meetings. This will usually be with your mentor, and should be formal (although they can be as casual as you both like, they must be scheduled, and convened with care). This is your opportunity to discuss any issues arising, and discuss them you bloody well must. Don't be a sap like me and keep things close to your chest, worrying that you'll look rubbish; you'll look rubbish when you're writing a book about it seven years later, that's when you'll look rubbish.

If the school hasn't explicitly offered you these processes and functions from day one, you have an absolute right to kick up a fuss – or perhaps more professionally, politely request when they'll be happening. This isn't troublemaking, it's simply asking for your entitlement as a teacher and a trainee.

My nerves were shot long before Christmas, and I couldn't bear the confrontation after confrontation that teaching seemed to demand. So I let most things slide, and if I set a detention, I only half expected them to turn up. And I was usually right. And if they didn't?

I just let it slide. Everything overwhelmed me; the next day there would be a flood of more detentions to set. Going home every night and trying to plan lessons was drowning me, and if I'm honest I had a lot of subject matter to catch up on. I can't blame my mentors; I was damned if I was going to present anything less than an exterior of humour and resolve. It was often commented that I looked like I was coping brilliantly, and that it seemed like I'd been teaching for years. There was no way that I could accept that I was an incompetent, even though the truth stared remorselessly at me every time I stared in the mirror.

The stress of it all seeped into every part of my life, and I'm not proud of how I acted throughout this period. Suffice it to say that for the best part of the year I was stressed more than I had ever been, and the worst bit was that

I didn't even realize it. I became aggressive, angry, tearful and sleepless and refused to admit anything was wrong. Friends, family and relationships all bore the brunt of my tailspin, I'm ashamed to say.

As a split-site school we moved about every single lesson; I inevitably found that I was missing one vital component a key, an exercise book, a wand, a jar of beating hearts. Something that would either bring everything to a halt, or at least make me look like 'that new teacher'.

Of course, this was compounded by the weight of the timetable. It wasn't at all like my training schools, where at least I had time to prepare, get books ready, mark, check I had resources, follow up on behavioural issues, meet deadlines etc. When the frequency of teaching got to a certain tipping point, it felt like an avalanche of work, and there was never enough time to clear it all; there was always something in progress that needed to be done that related to something that previously had been unfinished, until there was nothing but a white blur of tasks that rained down, one after another.

GCSE was another matter; not knowing about the Muslim beliefs about the afterlife meant I was buried in a pile of books every night, prepping myself with content, and hoping the skills would look after themselves. And A-level was something else entirely. Fortunate are you if your degree covered the topics you would be teaching at A-level; I certainly wasn't. I found myself buried in academic texts that I hadn't even seen at University (at which point I was a lot more diligent, I assure you). If it wasn't for the fact that I refused to regret anything, I would have regretted not preparing. A lot.

Getting ready

You may have gathered from this that content is best learned well in advance of lesson delivery. There's no excuse for not knowing what you're supposed to be teaching, none; after all, you came into the profession to impart something, didn't you? If it was only the vague belief that everyone has a beautiful candle inside them, then save yourself the trouble. My subject knowledge wasn't quite as bad as I'm sketching here, but it wasn't anything to be proud of either – there wasn't a lot of Mosques and Mandirs in my philosophy degree. But on the other hand, there's nothing in Key Stages 1–4 that you should have a problem with, assuming you have a reasonably relevant qualification, and assuming that you already possess relevant skills, the content you need to learn should be relatively easy.

Use your PGCE year, or your undergraduate time, or even your summer holiday prior to your first post to get your subject knowledge in order. On my PGCE we were given a checklist of relevant subject areas that we should be aware of, and like everyone else I bought myself some primers and read them. But that wasn't the same as learning it to a level where I felt confident to talk to a class about the teachings of Buddha, say. So before you start school, do yourself a favour and grab some of the school books you'll expect the kids to learn from. That should give you a clear idea of the content knowledge you'll need.

Fortunately school will always find ways to keep you busy; I was allocated duties in case I was getting drunk on all that free time during breaks and lunches. The duties basically involved standing in the playground or a lonely corridor, and either chasing children away from where you were standing or preventing them from knocking lumps out of each other. It was nice to be able to observe the kids letting off steam, and occasionally you'd get a brave (or lonely) one sidling up to have a chat. One of them was Robin, a difficult boy in my Year seven class who was a bit odd – the other kids gave him a lot of space. He sat next to me on the yard bench.

'Do you ever watch programs about Jesus and start to cry?' he said. Just like that, from nowhere. There was only one way I could answer without crushing him.

'Yeah, sometimes,' I said. Well, I'd just seen Mel Gibson's The Passion, and that put a lump in my throat, so I let it slide.

'I do,' he said. I got the impression he just wanted to tell someone about it, the poor kid.

'Nothing wrong with that,' I said. 'It's a sad story.' We just sat like that for a few minutes, and then he beetled off without a word. Sometimes it feels like there are oceans between people. And sometimes it feels like we have everything in common.

Relationships

That one conversation was more important than I thought; as Robin grew up through the school, he presented some pretty challenging behaviour to many teachers. But because of that initial, tiny point of contact, he always spoke to me with kindness and good manners. Never underestimate the benefit of building bridges with the kids.

This leads to another important part of behaviour management: getting to know the kids. This is a minefield for the new teacher, who is struggling to establish boundaries and ground rules for the children as well as for themselves. The best thing to say at this stage is that once you have established firm rules with the class, then you can develop that relationship by learning more about the students and personalizing your reactions to them. But far too many new teachers start trying to do this straight away and tie themselves in naughty knots with the kids. If they think you're too pally-pally at first, they'll think you're a soft mark. On the other hand, if you carefully and slowly build up human relationships with them based on tough love and sincerity, you can work miracles with them. Go slowly, start tough. Get to know them later.

One day in my Year ten class, Ade, an enormous shapeless boy who looked as though he should have left school three years previously (in more ways than one), took a Lynx spray out. I'm sure the ladies were swooning at the thought.

'Ade, put that away,' I said, 'I don't want you stinking the room out with that.'

'It's deodorant, man!' he said, correctly, as if that explained everything.

'Away. Now,' I said. He put it on the desk.

'Away,' I repeated.

'It's on the desk,' he said. You couldn't fault him.

I turned away, distracted by five other students starting to throw things at each other.

'Stop chucking stuff, you mongo!' said one girl, picking up her textbook and papers, and throwing them back in a flurry. Pens and more books followed. The rest of the class started bellowing in delight. Some chairs went over.

'Look at this!' Ade cried. In one hand he held the Lynx can. In the other he held a lighter, touching the nozzle to the head. The obvious thing happened, and a three feet arc of flame spread out over the desk. He sprayed off a few more bursts, and I marched towards him, shouting my head off. Then the bell rang, and everyone, including Ade, ran out, laughing their heads off. I was left alone in a room in chaos, chairs, tables and papers everywhere. I had no idea what I was supposed to do next. I still had no idea when my next class bustled in and started complaining about the mess. Some of them wouldn't come in because of the scorched, chemical smell that hung like a cloud in the room, and I spent the next ten minutes convincing them to come in, while inside the room students opened windows and sat where they liked.

When the lesson was over, I sat in the park near the school and smoked cigarettes for lunch. If I reported everything that was going on, I would look like a complete failure. But the more awful fact was that I didn't know where to start. There was so much misbehaviour going on in my lessons that it was nearly impossible to pinpoint who was misbehaving and who wasn't. I had been advised to keep a list of anyone who stepped out of line; the list was the class, probably, although I couldn't be sure because all I could see was the misbehaviour, and it occurred to me even then that I could barely see the ones who were working because of the chaff from the ones who treated my lessons like a games arcade.

It's not often that as an adult you get so ritually and repeatedly humiliated, at least not so overtly. It's compounded by the contrast between the role you are supposed to occupy (the authority figure, the guide and teacher) and where I was ending up (the clown, the joke). The human spirit can bear many things, but humiliation is one of the hardest things to carry. This carried on, and on, and on. There's an old story about boiling frogs: it's said that if you put a frog in a saucepan of cold water, and then slowly heat it, the frog doesn't notice the difference because the increase is so gradual; eventually the frog is boiled alive. I was starting to boil alive, and I couldn't even see it.

Christmas break couldn't come soon enough. Again.

Extreme behaviour

This is every trainee's nightmare. When you have a degree in Organic Chemistry, it's difficult to know what to do if someone chucks a chair out of the classroom, or creates a flamethrower (although a chemist could at least take advantage of the chance to explain the reactions taking place). No wonder; it's the kind of thing that usually the emergency services would deal with, not civil servants like teachers. And police get months of residential training in dealing with mentalists. Plus they have riot batons. We get a ten-minute lecture and a mug of coffee. Good luck.

If things kick off, there's no substitute for experience; once you've had a year or two worth of incidents like that, you won't be paralyzed in the moment when you're so stunned by the seriousness of the situation that you're stuck to the spot. What I should have done, of course, was order him to go to the Head's office, and if he refused (which was practically guaranteed), then leave the classroom (because it's an emergency) and summon senior management assistance; they can then deal with the situation. Something like the flamethrower, or a fight ... that can't wait till lunch time; that needs to be nailed instantly, otherwise people could get hurt, and that's priority number one.

Back to school in January, I braced myself. The weather was cold and dark, and with the celebrations of Christmas over, once again the year had *started on a cold and lonely note. Everyone was going down with viruses and ailments, real or psychosomatic. I felt like catching one myself or making one up. But at least it had given me a chance to recharge my cells, and I was braced to give it all another go. The worst thing about going back was the knowledge that it was going to be more of the same, and that I had merely forgotten how it felt to be crushed by the relentless classroom chaos. I barely gave detentions any more, because the misbehaviour was so prevalent that it was hard to see where normal ended and abnormal began. Besides, I had tried that route before: detentions, phone calls, meetings, warnings. None of it had worked; it only put a finger over the leak for a few lessons before another leak sprang up; stopping that one took me away from the first, which sprang up immediately I left. It was hopeless.*

Speaking of comedy, the new term saw me taking on a form group; although the school tended to keep NQTs away from this duty as a way to support their induction year, it was felt that as a FastTrack candidate, I was capable of taking on a pastoral role as well as a curriculum one. Well, I was doing so splendidly well, how could I refuse? This involved looking after a Year eight class first thing in the morning, registering them, getting them ready for the school day and acting as a liaison between the school and the home. They were, upon first meeting, a lively bunch.

Alas, a few of the kids in my form group were truly awful; a group of girls had formed a little gang, and leaned on each other for behaviour cues. They arrived late together, shouted to each other no matter where they were placed, and when told off separately, would smirk and look at each other and barely suppress their chuckles. When one behaved, the other two set themselves off like fireworks. Just getting them to do simple things like taking off their jackets was a trial, and I learned to my pleasure that even before I had taught my first lesson it was possible to be frazzled and exhausted; which was good because I was starting to think this teaching lark was a piece of p*ss, and I really needed something to bring my head down from the clouds and back to reality. And I was glad to see they were getting their cultural cues from East Coat rap/music videos (which someone once fabulously described as 'mildly pornographic adverts for money').

The role of a form tutor

Having a form class is exactly as demanding as you make it. If, like me, you were feeling too swamped to do anything other than babysit them, then a babysitter you shall be. To be honest I had no idea what else I was supposed to do other than tick their names off and have repetitive conversations with them about tucking shirts in and hiding their phones. I believe I was given a handout at some point, which I'm sure you'll agree is wonderful training and induction for a pastoral role.

The tutor is there to set an example for the students; to ensure they start the day in the right frame; to check their equipment, their planners and their appearance. These are small but significant factors to developing boundaries and routine with the children. It shouldn't be a chance for the kids to catch up, or to bring the playground into the school. It's a time to talk to them, to deliver messages and to discuss important school issues. The form tutor should also know if there are any significant curricular or pastoral issues with the children in school, so that they can assist in communicating these problems to other teachers and senior staff. Many tutors know the man that drives their bus better than they know their own form groups. Speak to the Head of Year for information about your class; look at their files; talk to them individually. It might not feel like it, but you'll start to become a significant adult in your life *if* you put the effort in to be one. And of course, if they mug you off in any way, treat it exactly like a lesson – you're still a teacher in a classroom, and more than that you're their form tutor – it means whatever you make it mean. So ask yourself what you want it to mean.

Campbell was perhaps the maddest boy in the whole of Year nine. So of course the Fates decided he would be with me for a year. The other kids were a bit frightened of him, even the other bad ones. They were merely naughty, but he looked like he would be setting ambulances on fire in a few years.

But curiously enough he seemed to like me; I didn't shout at him, because although I could fall into the trap of blowing my gasket, with him I realized that he had probably heard a lot worse in his life, and if that was all I had to offer, then I wasn't worth bothering about. One day we were looking at Buddhist funeral ceremonies (a real hoot) and he was doing his usual rap-babble to himself.

'Try this sheet,' I suggested, because I was paid to do so.

'Boo-boo-papp-paa-pa, bitches and hoes…' he replied poignantly.

'I like your rapping,' I said, lying easily. He stopped.

'You've got some talent in that area,' I said, like I signed artists for Motown. He looked around, and then showed me what he'd written in the back of his book, apart from the obligatory penises and non-work. It was full of rap lyrics (or 'flows' as I believe the hippity-hoppity people call it) which were actually much better than you would expect from a man who spent his class time picking his nose and wiping it on people.

'Very good,' I said, slightly more sincerely. 'But could you write about anything?' He made a face to indicate interest. 'Yeah,' he said.

'Could you write a rap about Buddhist funerals?' I said. Surely he wouldn't take the bait. Oh, but he did. Ten minutes later, I made an announcement to the class.

'Campbell has something to show us, so I'd like to ask you to be quiet.' I didn't have to ask twice; they feared him only as much as they humoured me. He spoke softly, like a small boy, and suddenly he looked the age that he was: not an enormous kidult, but a young man, a boy who was trying too hard to be an adult. It was actually quite good, and he'd covered more Buddhist material than some of the more diligent ones. When he finished I led the class in applause, and the bell went, which might have indicated my own poor timing, but punctuated the moment perfectly before anyone ruined it conspicuously.

It wasn't a break-through moment – this isn't a film – but it wasn't bad. In a sane world he would have been in a special school, but this isn't a sane world, and Campbell and his ilk are here for a while.

Teaching difficult classes

You can ascertain which kind of school yours is by reading the OfSTED report (but take it in context – many schools can pull a fast one with the mentalists just before OfSTED descend, so looks can be deceiving). Visiting the school is an acid test; if they behave well towards you as a stranger, if they conduct themselves well in public areas, and if you pass classrooms where order is the norm, you have a good idea of the character of the school. If they're chucking eggs at you from tower blocks, they're probably trying to tell you something.

I say this not to discourage, but precisely the opposite; teachers that enter the profession full of good intentions and high hopes are far more likely to get busted wide open as they realize all their love and aspirations mean nothing to some kids. But if you enter the profession loaded for bear[5] you can face the truth with courage. It can be tough as Hell at first, but that's part of the learning process, and if you know that's how it'll be I'll give you far shorter odds on making it as a teacher. This isn't a job for someone who can't think of

---

[5] I nearly said 'ready for a challenge', but I'm so weary of intolerable rudeness being described as a *challenge* that I'm banning that word from now on, because it sterilizes an experience more akin to a Premier League roasting than the cheery adventure it suggests.

anything else to do: sure, there are teachers by their thousands who fit into this category, and I sure wish they'd all grow some stones and leave, because they make the job worse for the rest of us, and they poison the lives of the kids they've got a duty to help flourish.

So grit your teeth and gird your loins, if you have any.[6] Some of these kids will put you through hoops. Don't worry. One day you'll be making some hoops of your own. Now, no book can tell you how to tame a class, because teaching is a verb, remember? You have to be in a classroom to learn how to do it, it's as simple as that.

1. Get the first impression right. I discussed this in a previous section. Make sure the first lesson you let them know that you're serious about behaviour. Some of them may slope in, look at you and laugh, or shout, 'Who are you?' while playing with themselves. Don't panic. Set your stall out and let them know what you expect.

2. Start to take names. Every time one of them crosses a line that you've drawn in the sand, you need to take down their names. Then you need to tell them somehow by the end of the lesson what their sanction is. Then you need to do it. Those three sentences contain the seed, the roots and the branches of good assertive discipline. They sound so simple, and I know how hard this is going to be for you, but you *need* to do them. If you have twenty-five kids on the naughty list, then twenty five it is. If they think they can get away with bad behaviour, they will. They will act exactly as badly as you let them. This isn't to say that it's your fault they behave badly – God save me from that piece of moronic logic – but that you are responsible for taming them. You can do it slowly like I did, or you can take the short cut, which I learned. The short cut is enormously hard work, for a long time.[7] But if you don't do what I eventually ended up having to do, you'll be repeating the same lesson forever. I mean it. Do you want to be herding cats for the rest of your career? Don't you want them to be taught instead? I thought so. Next step ...

3. Kick ass. Not literally. Do exactly what you said you were going to do. Usual sanctions are:

    ◆ sent out of lesson to cool down
    ◆ a warning

---

6   Loins, not teeth. Whatever.
7   And therefore, not a short cut at all. I lied.

- as short detention
- a long detention
- a phone call home
- a privilege revoked
- a meeting with parents
- an internal exclusion
- an external exclusion
- a permanent exclusion

One of the most common sanctions is the detention. Much has been written about this little fellow. I know that some schools operate 'no detention' policies, and jolly good luck to them. I'm sure there are some countries that have tried a 'no prison' judicial system, but they didn't last long either. Critics of detentions point out that they are a) boring b) punitive and c) unpleasant. I would add d) that's the point. If you don't like giving out sanctions then congratulations, you're still a human being. They are designed to be unpleasant; they have to be in order to act as a deterrent, which is what they are. The idea is that students will start behaving in order to avoid them. If they're fun and easy then they don't deter; they encourage. So while I sympathize with people (often parents) who feel that the time should at least be spent profitably if they are to be set at all, I would caution against them being too enriching. It's not a lesson – it's a punishment. And if lessons are punishing then maybe we need to take a look at them.

Set detentions. Set them in your break, at lunch, after school. Set them and do them.

4. If they fail to attend a sanction, or they continue to misbehave across lessons, then escalate. Move up the naughty step. You will probably need to involve more senior staff by this point; certainly your Head of Department, maybe a Head of Year, and so on. You should definitely have called the parents by this point. Would you want to know if your kid was misbehaving in lessons and ruining their education? No-brainer.

That, in a nutshell, is behaviour management. About half your classroom control is performed outside the classroom, after and before lessons. If you do this stuff – and it's not complicated – then you'll get 99 per cent of them eventually. Just persist, and never give up. Even when it doesn't seem to be working, it is; it's sinking in, even if it seems to be running off them like smoke.

Inside the classroom

So far I've mostly discussed structures and procedures to control behaviour. That's because it's your first priority. I'll say it again: until you have the class under control, you can kiss teaching and learning goodbye. Children aren't learning when they're mucking about, chatting, texting, mugging you off or sleeping. Honestly, they're not. And as a new teacher you'll be wading thigh-deep in resentment and simmering insubordination, so you'll need to fall back on the structures and rules. Once they realize that you're fair, consistent and aware of the school rules, they'll start to settle, albeit often in fits and starts, and slowly as molasses.

Here are some other things you can think about at the same time: they are skills rather than tips, and the best way to improve them is to observe others, have them observe you, and practise.

Body language. This simply means conducting yourself physically with dignity and grace. Act as if you expect to be obeyed, and if someone fails to do so, continue to act with dignity: look disappointed rather than angry; thoughtful rather than spiteful. Move slowly and with considered gestures, indicating gravity and seriousness.

Eye contact. Make it frequently, and with everyone. Hold a gaze for a second and then move on. It indicates fearlessness and confidence. Don't hold it for a pointless length of time, or they'll think it's a competition.

Rhetoric. Speak clearly and more slowly than you're used to. Use shorter sentences in order to be understood. Face the class as much as possible when you talk to them. Vary your pitch and tone so that you don't sound like a metronome. And keep the volume just slightly louder than normal conversation: only raise your voice when you're making a short instruction heard over background noise (and I suggest you make the instruction, 'Quiet, please.') You should almost never scream at the top of your voice, unless someone's safety is seriously threatened. It makes you sound out of control, emotional and weak. It might give them a shock the first time you do it, but once they've seen that these are your big guns, they know there's nothing left to be frightened of.

So keep control over your volume. If the class are too noisy for you to be heard then you need to act in way that reminds them to be quiet: repeat yourself; hold a hand up; clap your hands once; ring a bell; there are a million options that don't involve you ruining your vocal chords. Punish them, of course, for repeated noisiness. And, once you've got them reasonably quiet, don't forget the effect that lowering your volume can have on the class; if you become softer, they will often listen more closely to hear you, encouraged by the effect of intimacy that it creates.

Your judgement. Be calm and considered about the decisions you make in the room; if you appear to dither or make snap decisions, they will attempt to exploit your indecisiveness. Instead, think carefully and make the right decision. This will usually be a fair one. If it looks as though you can be swayed by kid pressure/whining/ wheedling/arguing/'pleases', then you will teach them to keep doing it. Once you decide something, stick to it, unless circumstances change. If you do have to change your mind, then do so with dignity. For instance, if you have wrongly accused a child, then apologize once, politely. Better still; don't make short, ill-tempered judgements. Be careful, and the kids will eventually respect you for your maturity – it's what they crave.

Keep your emotions under control. It's great to show passion and enthusiasm, but you need to show them that you're not going to make decisions based on how you're feeling, or that you're not going to be weird just because you're feeling a bit jolly. The kids need you to be a grown-up; they might kick and fuss and grin and jape, but you mustn't. You should be an even keel, someone they can rely on. If you're miserable, cheer up; if you're elated, shut up. Be a teacher.

All of these points are hard to 'do' just suddenly, but I mention them as things you can think about when you're reflecting on how to improve behaviour and build up a positive relationship with your classes. Practise them; pick one a time to observe or work on. See what works for you, not for me or anyone else. There are also a few bits and pieces you can think about to get better behaviour in the classroom, and by default, better learning:

Organising your room. The classroom is your space, not theirs; personalize it any way you want, if it will facilitate learning. By doing so, you also put your thumbprint on the room, saying 'This room is mine, not yours. The rules are mine.' Have them in rows, if you want maximum teacher attention, and minimal smirking at each other. You emphasize your role and position. Bit rubbish for group work though. Have a horseshoe, or an enormous tortoise, or small tables of six: whatever works for you. Experiment to see what you prefer.[8]

Seating. Get the nutters as far from each other as possible; keep friends apart. For God's sake, don't put the smartest kid next to the dullest child. It doesn't rub off, you know. By all means mix up the ability levels, cultures and genders, but no social experiments please. You're there to teach them, not to engineer them. Boy/girl pairs often work well due to the adolescent fear of the opposite gender. When you work out the seating plan keep an eye for diagonal neighbours as well as rows and columns. And change the plan if you want to; never give in to pressure to move from the children. If they move themselves move them back, and punish them for doing so. It's your room, remember ...

Rewards. Positive praise is a powerful tool to encourage and motivate; used prodigiously it becomes an accidental punishment, to you and them. Praise must go where it deserves, not just for doing what they should be doing anyway; by the same logic you might as well tell them off for behaving normally. Praise should be sincere, directed and specific. Some pupils love public praise, others would rather spend a weekend with Bruce Forsyth. Marking homework closely, with praise and comments, is a brilliant way to get to these kids. It's a private conversation between you and them; no one need know you're praising them. Letters home, phone calls home – these don't just have to happen for naughty things. If you do the same for goodness and effort, then you're doing the right thing.

Hint: if you've just done a lot of paperwork for naughty kids, take five minutes to write some merits/positive slips/postcards for the good kids, or the ones who have really tried. If you can do this then you'll remind them – and you – that it's not all about bad behaviour.

This last point is really important; you'll spend so much time dealing with misbehaviour that you'll start to think that's all the kids do. It's not. If you were honest with yourself then you'd realize that the majority of the kids you teach probably do the majority of what you ask, even if it's simple stuff, and that aberrant behaviour isn't the norm, its the annoying exception. The problem is that the misbehaviour is so obvious, so loud, so demanding of your attention that it appears to be nine miles tall and three miles wide. It's not. It's just bloody impervious to being ignored. There's a lot of goodness in

---

[8] Not too much. No pyramids, for example, not even in a maths lesson.

your room, just like there's a lot of good stuff in your teaching. We see the bad much more easily than the good, in our lives, in other people, in ourselves. Try to force yourself to see that, especially when things seem darkest, because that's when you need to realize it the most. And it's always true.

I know; easy, right?

As I was walking up the stairs to start my dreaded Year ten class I heard a commotion and a chanting that indicated two things; something entertaining was happening, and someone was getting their face filled in. This was unusual inside the building. I had broken up a few effete fights in the playground, and most of them were just about face, over some imagined slight. And most of them wouldn't happen if there wasn't an audience, cheering them on.

I rushed upstairs; inside, two whole classes crammed into my room, tables everywhere, and they bayed and whooped chaotically. Ade, the insane giant, was laying into the only other boy in the year who could equal him in height, although he was no match for his cruelty and casual violence. He was lying in a heap of chairs, as Ade launched punch after punch at him. He was enormous, well over six foot, and built like a bouncer. He was pasting the other boy, so I jumped in, as did another male teacher. The first thing I thought about was how to restrain Ade. I grabbed one of his enormous arms to stop it swinging; as I did so, the other teacher did the same on the other side. But Ade's massive strength wouldn't be thwarted by mere humans; like Godzilla, he lifted me physically in the air as he tried to get his fist into the boy's face. My weight managed to stop it becoming a punch, but I realized I was going to need a tranquilizer dart to take him down. The other teacher also lost his feet as Ade did the same with his other arm.

Enough being enough, we both bundled him onto the floor, and restrained him, which is something I hadn't done in years and never thought I'd have to do again. As a group of teachers took him downstairs, he shouted and snarled at his victim, who was led away to be smothered in ice packs and sirloin steaks.[9]

The lesson went quite well after that.

---

[9] Does that still happen? It did in the comics I used to read.

Fight club[10]

Unless you teach in a Catholic seminary, you'll meet a fight or two in your time. As I've mentioned, you are under no obligation to pile in like Jason Statham, and if it looks too hairy for you to handle safely then summon assistance and sleep with an easy conscience; it's a bit like tackling a fire, I suppose. On the other hand, if you feel that you can make a difference, and especially if someone else is getting clobbered, then you are perfectly within your rights to get stuck in. Keep your tactics to restraint and prevention, intervention and diplomacy. Hold arms back, push antagonists apart or – most satisfying of all – lift up the more belligerent little scrapper physically like something out of a cartoon. Using your fists would be practically unforgivable in any circumstance, unless you were actually being attacked yourself, or somebody was in danger of getting obviously seriously injured.

In most circumstances, the mere appearance of a teacher will be enough to dissolve a fight, although you need to make a big impact to get their attention. Plus they can't just stop immediately, otherwise they'll lose face, so if you're determined to break it up you'll probably need to wade in at least near to them and start laying on some hands. Be careful not just to jump in between them or you might get an accidental punch in the ribs. Be loud; announce your fearsome presence and start to slide yourself in; these things are best done by two teachers, because if it's a real fight and their blood's up, they might resist all attempts to be placated. If they've got the red mist then you need to tread carefully – but it's also important for you to get involved if you can safely, because in a real fight someone can get seriously hurt in a snap, by accident.

If it's a big blouse fight, more about saving face than anything else, then they'll jump at the chance to stop – just give them a reason by being there. Take care, but be aware that stepping into a fight is inherently risky, and there's only so much you can do to make it safe, so keep all the soft parts of your body covered. And put your mug down.

Year 11s were less openly contemptuous; they knew that exams were coming, and if I was what they had to work with then that was what they had. Especially after Christmas I noticed that they settled down much more quickly than the other classes; I had probably been putting more effort into my classes with them than with some of the others, because teachers feel the

---

[10] Rule 2: If it's your first year in teaching, you *have* to fight.

breath of exams on their necks too, and we had been constantly reminded of the importance of examination results to the school. It was the first sign I had that things could change for the better, and I started almost to look forward to going in to teach them. By the end of the second term, my classes with them were going well, and almost everyone was on task almost all the time. One or two loudmouths still openly questioned my ability to teach, but the rest of them had the manners not to join in. Some of them even expressed an interest in what I was teaching.[11]

The bottom set Year 11s were switching off rapidly. They were forced to be in a class that few of them could see any point in, and they were happy to tell me so.

'What's the point of this class?' they said.[12]

Still, by the second term, things had reached a plateau, by which I mean they weren't getting any worse. But I was still meeting the same defiance, the same faces, the same refusers, the same faces every time.

Something happened inside me; I realized that I couldn't give up. I refused to accept that I was going to be beaten by a bunch of fourteen-year-olds. I had spent ten years working with drunks, dregs and cross-dressers; I wasn't getting chased out of Dodge by people who couldn't legally buy fags. No matter how bad it was, I decided that I was going to stick it out as long as it took. I think the absence of an escape plan helped keep me on the straight, and by the third term I was glad I hadn't done anything stupid like pack it. I might be a rubbish teacher (no 'might' about it) but I was going to get better.

Motivating students

The benefits of motivating them are obvious – if they want to do something then they'll do it without you having constantly to light rockets under their collective asses. Plus they'll enjoy it. What are the alternatives to incendiary-based incentives?

Make the lessons interesting and enjoyable. Piece of cake, I realize. Still, because you're a human being you intrinsically know the difference between something boring and something interesting. This could mean many things: talk passionately about your subject; have lots of different activities; plan well; don't just resort to constant book work; get them engaged using all their senses; play games with educational outcomes; show interesting media and get them to

---

[11] Fancy that.
[12] See?

discuss it; have competitive elements to your lessons ... there are a million things to make your lessons more enjoyable. Some kids switch off from lessons that were clearly planned on the back of an envelope on the way from the bathroom. Mind you, some of them would sit still if you stood at the front and read the telephone directory. But I'd advise against that, especially if OfSTED are stalking the corridors like the Dark Riders.

Rewards. If you incentivize them externally to the subject itself, you might (repeat: might) get them to associate the subject with the benefits you bring them. Rewards can be tangible, like sweets and treats; they can be human rewards, like praise, merits, stars in their books, phone calls home or anything they desire and you can supply. The more sparing you are with your rewards, the more valuable they are;[13] give them out fairly and only when they are deserved, otherwise you look just as unfair as a bully, but you also look soft as well as unfair.

Punishments. The other end of the carrot/stick equation. People will do a lot more to avoid discomfort than they will to pursue a distant pleasure, so do what educators have done for centuries and set mousetraps for behaviour you don't sanction. Any time they cross the line, let the executioner's axe fall on them. This will be one of your most common strategies, I'm afraid, because many, many children just can't see the point of trigonometry, continental plate drift or the Book of Acts, I'm afraid to say. I know, crazy, isn't it? Part of your job is coercion, like it or not. If you wait for them to work because they want to, then I suggest you pull up a chair because you'll be waiting for some time.

Passion. An essential part of a teacher's arsenal. You should love your subject, even the boring bits, because it's part of the bigger picture. If you're teaching because you can't think of anything better to do, then shame on you, because your job isn't just to grumble at kids and wish you were somewhere else; you should be teaching because you love working with kids and love your subject. Or if you're not, you should be in love with the idea of helping kids get ahead in life. After all, if you're not motivated, I fail to see why the kids will be – and they'll fail to see it too. In all things, convey the idea that your subject is interesting, relevant and high status. If you walk

---

[13] *I could teach economics.*

into a lesson and sigh, 'Well, I suppose we have to learn this – sorry it's boring,' then the kids will switch off before you can say 'Happy slap'. And you'll deserve it.

Motivation is a tricky thing – you'll have to use the whole range of suggestions above, and combine them all at once to get the maximum effect. But you won't get them all motivated, remember that. Some times you have to accept that you won't win every battle. You can, of course, try; some pupils just need time to realize your subject is life-changing. Some never will. That's why we have detentions.

The salary was certainly helping. Although I wouldn't be ordering home-delivered, truffle-coated lark's tongue from Harrods' any time soon, I was no longer buying ten-packs of Mayfair Blue or living off kidney bean risottos.[14]

One of the things I had been dithering about was whether or not to sign up to the teacher pension, because if I didn't then I'd be up about a ton every month, which sure sounded like a lot less kidney beans to endure to me. Fortunately I had enough people around me who actually knew which way up a fiver went to stop me from doing the obvious, stupid thing, and I stayed in the scheme. I just had to close my eyes to the prospect of easy instant cash, for the warm glow that a protected state retirement package can provide.[15]

The second term ticked by; I saw other teachers coping even less well than I was, and for a second it took the edge off my feeling off perpetual defeat. Only for a second: Schadenfreude can only sustain you for so long before your own Weltschmerz kicks back in. There was, of course, more to come, just in case I was starting to feel smug.

---

[14] I no longer want to see a kidney bean as long as I live.

[15] And Holy Moly, am I glad I did. The only way you'll get a better pension is by discovering oil in your back garden when you hit 60. Pensions terrify anyone under the age of, oh, 59. Luckily everyone knows that they'll live forever …

9 | Cannons to the left, marking to the right: *Adventures beyond the classroom*

'HEY! I DON'T THINK HE'S A REAL TEACHER!'

STATUS .

I sat at my first parents' evening with a long list of who I was meeting, and a diary open at my attendance and homework page for the Year nine class. It wasn't much to go on, and I was feeling a bit naked.[1]

The first parents arrived, and mum and dad fell into their chairs. Both of them were wearing sweat trousers and T-shirts that indicated attendance at the West Point Academy gymnasium.[2] From the look of them, they hadn't been in a while. West Point Dad ran a hand over his shiny scalp and made a grimace.

---

[1] And not the kind I like, either.
[2] Which was incredible, as I didn't think any of the parents would have been to such a prestigious American Military University.

'How long will this bloody take?' he said with a pained tone. 'EastEnders is on later.'

Parents. You have to love them.[3]

But that kind of lardy, unlovely parent was by far the exception; the ones who had bothered to come to the evening obviously cared enough about their children to forego EastEnders (for the most part). If that sounds like the lowest expectation in the world ever, you're probably right. But I enjoyed my first parents' evening immensely. It was a stream of mums, dads, elder brothers, aunties (it's confusing; I learned pretty sharpish not to assume it would be Mum and Dad in front of me. My favourites were when an older brother, maybe two years above the kids at school was sent to represent for the evening. Boy, the nuclear family should be in a museum).

I found it charming; I saw some parents piling into teachers across the room from me, angry abut this comment or that comment, or imagined slights against their children. This never happened to me; maybe all those years behind bars had paid off.

By the end of it, I had talked almost constantly for about three hours, due to the fact that parents never wanted to sit snugly into their time slots (amazingly they had five minutes allocated to discuss everything), so we overran into the late evening. But at least, dry as my throat was, it felt like I had contributed to something. And I had finally got the chance to meet a lot of the parents of the children who had been having such fun in my lessons.

After that, I started to notice a fractional change in some of their behaviour. I say fractional; you would need an electron microscope to detect. But I could see it, and when I saw the kids next, I could say, 'I spoke to your parents and had a lovely conversation', and mean it.

Parents' evenings

This is one of the best opportunities you can have for building up relations with the home. Why is this so important? Because if the parents support your teaching, you've brought learning home. Few children will misbehave or girn unattractively at you if they know that their parents will descend on them like the Abyssinian hordes when they get home, because between school and home, they have nowhere to hide. But the converse is equally true: if you lose the sympathy of the parents you might be dealing with little Sammy's belligerence until Judgement Day. So it makes huge, perfect, glorious

---

[3] Oh no you bloody don't. I checked my contract.

sense to make a meaningful contact with the parents or guardians of the students; and parents' evening is the perfect place to do it.

So your attitude to the evening must be positive. It's an opportunity, not a chore, despite the obvious loss of the occasional evening you endure. Here are my best tips for making them work:

◆ Stand up when they enter and shake their hands. Tell them how nice it is to see them, and thank them for coming in. If that sounds obvious then it's because it is. But I am amazed to see teachers not doing this. Such a simple courtesy, effortlessly creating an atmosphere of warmth and conviviality.

◆ Start with something positive about the pupil; everyone, no matter how unlovely, has something nice to be said about them. 'Charlie's been an interesting boy to teach,'; 'Ama has made some great contributions to debates,' etc. Charlie and Ama might have the mark of Beelzebub tattooed on their foreheads, but do this; make an effort. Few are the parents who think their child is the naughty rascal that he or she might appear to be in school; so if you start with something negative ('Your son is disgusting') then the parents will instantly be defensive.

◆ Have some meaningful data available. You should be able to say something about their attendance, punctuality, equipment, progress, behaviour, current grade and prospects. The more evidence you have to support this, the easier it is to convince the parents if there is a problem.

◆ Have some bookwork to show the parents. This is a great technique, because it is indisputable (see: data, above). The parents can see how well or not little Shelley is doing by the quality of work she produces. If the work is poor, it's an interesting talking point, and the parent is usually shocked. It's often useful to have a great pupil's work to show by way of contrast.

◆ Be aware of any specific difficulties the pupil may have. If you have a go at Robin or Ray for sloppy handwriting or spelling, and the parent says, 'But didn't you know he's dyslexic, blind and has no hands?' then you will look exactly like the pillock you are. Same goes for more able children; be aware of the gifted and talented register, and make sure that you know the pupil needs different challenges.

◆ It might sometimes look as though you have nothing in common with the parents, but I guarantee you do: the well-being of the student. If you say, 'We both want the best for Daniel,' then you tacitly create rapport between you and the parents because it's something they can't disagree with. You do want the best for Daniel, right?

Report time came up too, too quickly. The school was obliged to communicate with the parents/home to let them know how their little lovelies were doing, and that meant writing reports.

I found that if I wrote as fast as I could, I could do a class in about an hour and a half. If you had two or three classes in the year group you could say good bye to a whole evening. Since I reserved my evenings for bouts of tearful self-recrimination interspersed with bouts of melancholy, I felt cheated. Then I had the indignity of getting them sent back to me from above with comments like 'expand' or 'more detail'. I longed for the days of 'VG'. Comments also had to conform to a certain style, which took a little longer to identify. For example, it was no longer considered good form to describe a pupil as 'lazy' or 'annoying', even though it might be patently true. Such terms, I was informed, were heavy with value judgements, and liable to offend.

Similarly, when describing 'ways forward', obvious pieces of advice like 'stop mucking about' and 'actually do some bloody work' were no longer done. They were replaced with 'needs to make a consistent improvement in his effort' and 'struggles to access the syllabus.' Man, who farted? Reports were printed and checked, and printed and checked again. I dreamed of a day when computers were doing this kind of work, since we weren't allowed to be particularly expressive. In my placement schools I had seen comment banks on the computer, where the teachers just clicked on a range of approved expressions, sentences and judgement-free judgements. I didn't realize it at the time, but I looked back on that like a dog remembering the day it got a bone.

Writing reports

This one's a bit harder to sell as a great opportunity, although it still is. Writing reports is undeniably one of most teachers' least favourite party games; they are time-consuming, laborious and painstaking. They are also an important part of your job, so the simple answer to any grumbles must be 'tough'. They are a legal requirement on the school, and an important organ of home/school communication. But they can also be seen as an opportunity to create a relationship between you and the family, and let them know about things that concern or delight you, and communicate ways forward in all cases. Under no circumstances use the report card as an opportunity to

SCHOOL SUPPORT FOR NEW TEACHERS,

'DO YOU NEED SOMETHING FOR THE OTHER HAND?'

settle scores with children; it's deeply unprofessional, and a little pathetic for an adult to act this way. If the behaviour's been bad, then it can be said in an unemotional and businesslike way. Besides, if the behaviour has been bad, then the parent should know about it already. I've already mentioned the importance of phoning home, and while many teachers balk at this task, I cannot recommend it highly enough as a behaviour management/teaching and learning tool. If you're not talking to the parents, you're missing an enormous trick, believe me. Get it right and you've got the strength of ten.

So when you write reports, see it as a chance to say things that are thoughtful, helpful and honest. Write professionally, because that's what you are, or what you're trying to convey. Don't whine, or bitch or snip. Don't gush either; unless a child is the Platonic ideal of dedication, manners, compassion and wisdom, there is always room for improvement, and the most talented children don't benefit from empty praise that gives them no direction about how to progress. Of course, you can use it as an opportunity to let the parents know if they've been great, but don't forget the ways forward.

Some schools use comment banks: IT-led responses to the reports that can be generated quickly from a database of pre-written sentences. This is faster, and removes the need for the reports to be spell checked; it also loses a degree of personalization. Other schools ask their teachers to write personal comments, which can make the report individual, but takes longer and is more prone to mistakes. Such schools usually have a style guide, which will range from a light touch to draconian restrictions. Whatever your school does, follow it. Resist the temptation to cut and paste enormously, as it shows that you either aren't aware of the pupil's individual circumstances, or that you don't care. Of course, it might also indicate you're enormously busy, which you undoubtedly are, but such admin tasks are still your responsibility, so until robots write them for us, we're stuck with them. Get some time and space, get your head down and get them done.

Meetings started to figure in a large way in my life at school. Department meetings were cosy, as we talked about classroom stuff: what we were teaching, and trips, and visits, and resources, and all the stuff that runs a classroom. And of course, every time we were asked how it was all going, I would stoically say, 'Fine' and do the Clint Eastwood thing again. I got so good at it, and I kept my kids so firmly in my lesson (rather than send them out the room and let them go crazy in the corridors – I was nothing if not considerate in my inadequacy) that I had earned a solid reputation as 'that new guy who's doing well'.

Year team meetings were more concerned with pastoral matters: we discussed who was being excluded; whose parents were divorcing; who was caught with stolen property; where the year group was going on a trip, etc. Fortunately my Head of Year/Learning was an old hand who despised meetings as much as we did; they were over in about ten minutes flat and then he would drag us over the road to the pub to tell us stories about being an ex-police frogman.[4]

Staff meetings were the most exciting bit of theatre on the calendar. The Head Master still followed the traditional format where everyone would cram into a tiny room, he would announce what he was planning to do at the school, and then people were invited to comment and debate it. Of course there was always an awkward squad willing to go ten rounds with any new initiative that came up, and for the majority of us, staff meetings were a chance to sit back and watch the fireworks. There was an enormous feeling at the end that nothing had been achieved apart from people having a chance to moan a bit and huff and flounce.

I noticed that some of the older members of staff would roll their eyes knowingly whenever anything new was rolled out. They would always say, 'Oh that again,' like it was gastric reflux. It took me a while to realize what they meant; at the time I just thought they were being mean and reactionary.

---

[4]   Brian Samways, I salute you.

Meetings

School love meetings. I think they fancy them. What else can explain the relentless diet that forms the backbone of the post-teaching period, and keeps you in long after the last teenager has left the building? Year teams, staff training, INSET, whole school meetings, form teacher meetings, curriculum meetings ... a seemingly endless spectrum to stop you getting home before dark. Most of them will be compulsory; in your first year the school will deliver 'essential'[5] induction information to you, although they might seem a tiresome task or a pleasure depending on the quality of delivery. Endure, regardless; they are compulsory and vital evidence that you have met the standards of induction.

Be on time, and be prepared. Sounds obvious, but the majority of teachers, even if they arrive on time, will only have a vague idea about what the meeting is about and why they are there. This is fine if you want to be a passive observer, and maybe in your first year of teaching you could be excused for doing so. But if you want to start earning respect among other people, and if you want to be noticed as someone who cares about teaching, doesn't want to be dictated to and wants to develop and learn, then turn up with something to say. Some meetings are very autocratic, and there won't be much opportunity to discuss, but most of them give you the opportunity to provide some input. Listen, take notes and contribute. Even if you say something stupid, you can still learn something. If you want to be a professional, you can't be a bystander in your own job. Get involved.

If the meeting is more prescriptive, then listen and learn. If someone has the power to force you to a meeting, then whatever they have to say to you could be important; if you want to be kept up to date about what the school is up to, what's going on in education or what direction the curriculum is taking, take a pen and paper and write it down. Schools are awash with data and the best way to keep on top of it all is to write it down – not so you remember it, but so you can forget it, and refer back to it when you need to. See note taking as a replacement for memory; a hard copy for when you need to know something consciously. Try it.

If you attend an INSET[6] then you will probably be asked to endure a lot of sugar paper and felt tip pens. You will be lectured to for a short

---

[5] Irony commas.
[6] In School Service and Training. Hellish.

while, and then usually asked to 'reflect on what you have learned' at the end of the day. This will probably involve a brainstorm, or as it used to be called, 'talking to each other'. If you are lucky, you will be asked to 'share best practice' which is another phrase for 'talk to each other about what you know already'. This makes it difficult to 'reflect on what you have learned.' If you are even luckier, the building will collapse and you can go to hospital to receive treatment for mild concussion, thereby avoiding the whole thing.

I ask you to endure.

Time management

You will become incredibly busy as a teacher. You may see teachers loafing around the staffroom as if they have nothing to do. They do; they're just not doing it. Nobody at school has spare time; even the squirrels in the playground are holding down two jobs. If people are doing their jobs right, they'll be occupied from clock on to clock off. This is something that has to be accepted when you enter the profession. What you don't have to accept is that you'll always feel like there's too much to do, or that you're swamped by the demands placed on you. As an NQT you will feel this more than most of the staff, not less, which is why some allowances are made for your time. Looking after yourself, and using efficiently, the time that you do have is essential.

♦ **Organize yourself**. Use a diary/planner and for the first year, make it your best buddy. Write down everything that is coming up, and everything you need to accomplish. Make sure you look at it before you retire every evening so you can be sure you're ready for the next day.

♦ **Make to-do lists**. Do this every day, and cross them off as you knock them off.

♦ **Prioritize**. What needs to be done now, and what can wait until later. Do the former first, obviously. Don't put off unpleasant jobs until you have to do them, otherwise they prey on your mind.

♦ **Learn to say *no***. This is tough, but you're going to have to start. Many people will make demands on your time, often innocently. They'll ask if 'you can just ...' do lots of things. It's great to help, and you must, in order to be both a good colleague and a human being, but learn to smell a rat. Some people will ask you to help because they're being lazy. Some will genuinely need help. The question is, what do *you* need? Your first year is supposed to be about you developing as a teacher and flourishing in your role. If the jobs of others start to erode that experience, then you're not doing the right thing. This is especially tricky if you are, by nature, helpful. Put yourself first a bit. You can even say to them, 'Of course I'll help you; let's see ... I can meet with you on Wednesday at three.' You've shown willing, but also indicated that your time is valuable and not given to the whims of others.

◆ **Schedule time with yourself.** If you know you have three classes of marking to be done, and you have two hours non-contact time on Wednesday, then this is an appointment you make with yourself. If someone says, 'I see you're free on Wednesday; I'd like you to take some kids to Tibet,' or something, then you can truthfully say, 'Sorry, but I'm busy.' And you are; busy with stuff you need to do. Resist the temptation to feel bad.

◆ **Accept you are human.** If things start to get on top of you, don't think, 'Gosh, I'm rubbish,' think, 'Gosh, I appear to be busier than the laws of physics allow. Something's gotta give.'

◆ **Something's gotta give.** Connected to all the previous suggestions is the idea that you need to face facts: if you can't do everything you think you have to in the time available, then you need to check your priorities, and consider if all your tasks are essential, important, desirable or irrelevant.

◆ **Don't walk alone.** There are other people at school, you know. If you need help, ask someone else if they can help – in the first instance it should be your line manager or the person in charge of the task you're performing. Tell them your concerns. It doesn't make you look rubbish, it makes you look professional. 'I'm concerned I won't be able to meet deadline x,' you can say, 'What advice/help can you give me?'

◆ **Don't take too much home.** It is inevitable that some work will leak home with you as an NQT, and you'll probably find planning more comfortable at your own desk. But I recommend that you do as much at school as you can, and save your home time as a space to relax in. This isn't just to keep you sane (which is important enough), but to keep the quality of your professional output high. You are no good to anyone if you're fagged out, depressed, stressed and tired. Except a shrink.

Being new to the school guaranteed me what seemed like a lifetime of being observed; it felt like a weekly event, but in reality it was far less frequent than that. As part of the support offered by the school, I would be observed in a variety of settings and year groups to make sure I wasn't teaching them witchcraft, or handing out cigarettes. I took it very seriously. This was my first series of milestones at school, and the secret garden of my classroom was about to have its door opened. It's funny how isolated you can feel as a teacher at the same time as hundreds of children and scores of adults are buzzing around you only metres away; it must the loneliest job you can do in a crowd.

Usually I would be given a week's notice, and had to write a lesson plan, for which there was a standard template; at times filling this out felt like an act of pure fiction. I knew roughly what I would be doing, and in what order, but I had no idea if it was what anyone was looking for, so I trusted my intuition and hoped for the best.

I looked at my watch about twenty times in those lessons, and felt like I'd climbed Everest if I had them all standing up behind their desks when the bell rang. In the course of a year I went through this process several times; in those days the teacher wasn't given a grading on their lessons, just feedback. I was pleased to hear that whatever I was doing, it was doing OK, because all I ever heard were positive comments and encouragement to try a few things differently here and there. I was amazed; I thought it was all falling apart for me, and that at any moment I would be uncovered as the worst teacher in the UK, officially, before I was turfed out back into the void. Even more amazing was how my classes behaved; strangely, for every observation lesson I had my classes would behave beautifully; not perfectly, but the best they could be with me. A wise owl told me something that I could hardly believe.

'They must like you,' he said. 'If they like you they want you to do well when you're being observed. If they don't they tear you up for toilet paper.'

They liked me. I felt like Sally Field when she won best actress.

Half way through the third term the school got a phone call that was the educational equivalent of a nuclear alert: OfSTED were coming to pay us a visit. Suddenly the whole school tightened its bowels. The amount of stress felt was directly proportional to the height you climbed in the hierarchy; the senior staff looked like geese on Christmas Eve. Down in steerage class, my fellow trainees and I were already wound up, stressed and exhausted, so an imminent visit from Her Majesty's Inspectorate made little difference. We were used to people poking their noses into our classrooms and making snooty notes on clipboards, written lesson plans and sleepless nights, so it was business as usual. Suddenly, children vanished from the school; not abducted by the grey aliens, but coincidentally and fortuitously temporarily relocated to the internal exclusion unit, where they could harm no one but themselves. I always wondered how lucky it was that the 5 per cent of mentalists did a disappearing act just before the inspectors came in, and returned immediately they left. Life's funny like that.

For three or four days we were invaded by strangers in mid-range M&S suits, who carried clipboards and briefcases; everywhere they went a senior staff member shadowed them like a fruit fly, and I could imagine teams of painters and decorators preceding them everywhere. We were told to be on our best behaviour; all lessons were to be planned and submitted in advance; everything about our paperwork was checked and checked again. In the end, they came, saw and conquered without bothering any of us, and I must say I felt a bit let down that they hadn't sneaked into one of my lessons, with Campbell rapping about Muslims and Ade setting fire to aerosols. They missed a show.

Observations and OfSTED

Ah, the dreaded OfSTED, the Scylla and Charybdis of teaching. The prospect of a visit terrifies many teachers, which is odd, because as OfSTED are fond of saying, they're there to observe the kids and support the school. Of course, the kids don't have to do much preparation and planning, and nothing much happens to them if things don't go well. Teachers get clobbered. As soon as the call comes in that OfSTED are visiting, the school adopts a siege mentality. You'd think the Vikings had been spotted in the distance. Some schools cancel trips and leave, as if they wanted to pull the drawbridge up

'HEY, EMILY. THIS BOOK ON CIVIL RIGHTS DOESN'T SAY ANYTHING ABOUT MOBILE PHONES. I THINK IT'S BROKEN!'

RIGHTS.

and start heating up the pitch and oil. It's unlikely as a trainee teacher that you'll get an OfSTED inspection in your first year, but unlikely is a long, long way from impossible.

At this point you have to know that the vast majority of schools takes them very seriously indeed. If they judge the school to be unsatisfactory in any major aspect, the school will be put into special measures, which will in turn incur more rounds of inspections and close scrutiny by the LEA and central office. If the school underperforms through successive observations, it can even be closed down.

Of course the major outcome of an OfSTED inspection is the production of the OfSTED report, which is freely available online and available to scrutiny by anyone who is interested, from potential job applicants to prospective parents and their children. In other words, a bad report can switch the tap off for good recruits and parents who want the best for their children. Some say this becomes a self-fulfilling prophecy, and creates 'sink' schools where parents leave a school in droves because of a negative report, which reinforces the reasons why the school ... but I said I wouldn't rant.[7]

The people who really lose weight over an OfSTED inspection are the senior staff. It's like the Second Coming for them. Trust me; in the run up to an inspection, they will not have a sense of humour. But from your point of view, there's not a lot to worry about; as a trainee you are expected to be on a learning curve and no one expects you to pull a circus lesson out of your hat. In fact, given that you will be undoubtedly already producing lesson plans, and used to observers, there isn't a huge amount of difference from your normal procedure. Just relax, try not to mop up everyone's anxiety, and do what you do. Others will be having grand mal seizures, but you don't need to. The inspectors will only see a fraction of lessons while they are there anyway; there's a team of three or four, and they usually stay no longer than a few days. Do the maths; there's a good chance they'll never step foot in your classroom. Don't bet on it though. If they do come in and you haven't planned a lesson, you will deserve all the torment that will follow. When I said relax, I didn't mean fall asleep.

---

[7] And I shan't even mention the suitability of the inspectors themselves. Did you know that it used to be standard practice to have a 'non-expert' observer in every team, i.e. someone who has never actually worked in a school? That's nice, isn't it? I think I'll start hanging about in cardiac surgery theatres and start writing reviews of surgical procedures. Oh yes, I forgot, that would be retarded.

The only contact I had with the Local Education Authority was a series of induction INSET days that I and my rookie buddies were sent on. To get there we trudged through a grey estate of post-modern buildings and tenements that the Luftwaffe had kindly cleared space for, ending up in a converted Victorian school that had been turned into a municipal community centre and professional training unit. It looked and felt as warm and human as it sounds. There, we had to endure the most excruciating training that I have ever endured (and remember that I worked for a large leisure and retail company in a previous life). Imagine, if you will, the sight: twenty-five trainee teachers in their first year, sitting around tables facing each other. A PowerPoint glows menacingly in the background. Pens and sugar paper lie on the tables like torture instruments. Then, after a short pep talk about how wonderful it must be to be new teachers, we grit our teeth and go through the 'getting to you know' you bit. Then we share our experiences with each other for about an hour. Then we feed back to the class.

Then, just when it can't get any worse, we share best practice. Sugar paper is involved, and wasted. Then we feed back our findings to our colleagues. Inside me, something dies. This then goes on for a few more hours until my spirit is entirely crushed. We get given a biscuit and then we're released, like prisoners, back into the world. Some of us, I'm sure, don't make it.

Maybe those training days were the low point of the year. I left them knowing less about teaching than I did before; it was like magic.

I was now better at getting the mentalists out of the classroom. A wise old owl had told me that if someone was persistently disrupting the lesson, then why wasn't I getting them out?

'Because I thought the point was that we were supposed to be trying to teach them all,' I answered. 'If we send them out then they don't get a chance to learn.'

'They aren't learning anyway!' he said, amazed. You need to get them outside or away if you want anyone to learn at all. How do you think the other kids in the class will learn anything if you don't sort out the ringleaders?'

And he was absolutely right. I could look back over two terms of madness in my classrooms, and while I don't think I would call it perspective, not yet, I could definitively start to see patterns. I was still trying to teach everyone, slavishly believing that they all had a right to be taught. What I hadn't seen was that by keeping them all cooped up together, I was ruining it for dozens of other kids. So I started focusing on the ring leaders in the classroom, the real instigators. I took, if not a zero tolerance approach to them, at least a low tolerance approach. I knew when they were building up to serious misbehaviour, so started to focus all my energy on putting them out of the game as soon as they started to blow up.

It was a small start, but a start nonetheless.

Judith and I took a group of more able children to the Hindu temple in Neasden. As I spoke to them on the trip, I realized that for many of them, the school trips were the only chance they had to go anywhere special, or anywhere exotic or far away. The economic mix of the school was wide; some of them came from families of professionals and double incomes, multiple foreign holidays and lifts to school; others wore the same shoes all year round and into the next, smelling of smoke and handing their free school meal vouchers over with either nonchalance, pride or anxiety, depending on their perspective. It felt good to be involved in taking children to see things that they would never normally see, and as I saw them ooh and aah at the splendid carvings of the enormous white marble Mandir, I knew that these were the moments that, for some, would remain. One girl said, 'I want to be a Hindu!' when she saw the beautiful statues; I wasn't sure how her Pentecostal mother would take it,[8] but it was quite an accolade.

They're called trips for a reason

It will be unusual for you to be asked to plan and execute a trip solo in your first year, but you may well be asked to participate in one; if you are asked, accept. Trips are an excellent way to learn more about how the informal curriculum works, and how to look after kids outside the classroom. It's also a great way to form relationships with pupils; if they can see that you're looking out for them and want you to be safe, then they seem to transfer a small degree of parental authority to you. They are, after all, children, and will look to you to keep them safe and happy. Finally, it's often a nice way to spend a day, especially if it involves an activity you find interesting, or a subject at school you know nothing about (so you can pinch their ideas[9]).

There is a far bigger responsibility though; as a teacher taking pupils out of the relatively controlled biosphere of the school, you expose them (and yourself) to a range of unknowns and potential hazards. Some of them are obvious, like busy roads and stranger danger, and some less so (has your diabetic/hay feverish/allergic child remembered her insulin/antihistamine/Epi-pen? Would you know what to do?). Some things only become dangerous when you involve large groups of children; we can all imagine the hazards of

---

[8] Calmly, I'm sure.
[9] It's not called stealing in education; it's called 'sharing best practice'. It's stealing, but you're allowed.

getting on a tube or bus – slight, but present. But you try getting fifty pupils at once on to a carriage or bus. Suddenly it doesn't look so easy.

Oya was throwing another tantrum in my form room; the object of her ire was, as usual, me, and my predictable unfairness towards the Human Rights of young people, as guaranteed by … well, nowhere, actually, but she was bloody sure they existed. The problem today was the fact that she thought she should be able to wander around the room as she pleased. Clearly I couldn't see her intrinsic right to do so, and for my failure to honour her nomadic soul she was trying to give me an earful, but because she was a screechy midget it came across like a dwarf getting boiled. I'd had enough of this. Later that day I called home and explained that their daughter was approaching critical mass for rudeness and selfishness. Her parents listened gravely, and I at least felt like I'd gotten it off my chest. I knew she'd been having problems across the board, so it wasn't just me this time. Ten days later I walked into my classroom to be greeted with her absence. I learned that her parents had decided that it wasn't working out for her over in the UK, and she had been sent back to central Africa until she learned some manners. Now that's a sanction.

My Year eleven bottom set had reached a strange point; many of them had started to ask for revision notes, and in lessons, most of them at least made a stab at the work I was setting, although nobody was going to win any prizes for busting their asses. Perhaps they had noticed that the exams were rushing towards them? I wonder what gave it away? Oh yes: the calendar. I realized that things have to be awfully close before some teenagers will notice them. The other third of the class were clearly ready to give up, but rather than turn that apathy into anything mean or nasty, they just turned it to … well, apathy. I guess apathy doesn't fuel anything in the long run, unlike say, rage or jealousy.[10] *Some of the kids fell into a truce state with me; they sat with their heads on the desk for half the lesson and I basically let them, interrupted rudely only by me occasionally saying, 'C'mon John, make a bit of an effort, eh?' Even then I felt a bit rubbish letting them get away with it, but I could see that they had completely given up, and I was glad that they weren't actively dancing on tables and ruining it for everyone else.*

Which raised another point: I was almost sympathetic to their point of view. John was leaving school in three months to start training as a plumber with his Dad; James was off to join the army as soon as he could leave school. Others had similar ambitions, or none at all; the reason for them to revise the five pillars of Islam or the six causes of world poverty eluded them, and I'm

---

[10] It's the emotional state that can't quite get its sh** together.

not sure I caught them in any grand fashion. Although it was undoubtedly not 'best practice' I allowed some of them to tune out, and for the first time that year I had quiet classes where the students wanted learn, and I wanted to give them everything I had. Even the Year ten class had started to follow a pattern of sitting down and more or less getting on with it.

Work/life balance

This brings me to another very important topic: you. This isn't an invitation for us to sit around a camp fire, hug each other and weep. This is me acknowledging that you are a human being with finite amounts of time, potential, energy and ability. No matter how capable you are, you will have limits. Throughout your first year in schools you will meet these limits, I guarantee you. Get to know them. Give them cute names.

This is step one to not going insane; recognizing that you cannot do everything; that you will fail sometimes; that you will make mistakes, forget things, let someone down, look stupid, lose something important. You will feel tired – exhausted, even. Sometimes you will feel as if your head will explode; that you're the worst teacher in the world, that you're letting everyone down, that you can't cope. You may even feel tortured by emotions you can barely name, conflicts of anger, guilt, depression, frustration and sadness.

This is normal.

Step two is recognizing it when it happens. This is the harder bit; one of the Catch-22 aspects of this situation is that when you feel like any of the above, you fail to realize that you are reaching the end of your tether. This is the point when some people keep on going, and end up exhausting themselves, falling into depression, burning out or even quitting. It helps if you have a good friend outside of school you can confide in. It also helps if you have someone in school looking out for you, and who speaks to you on a regular basis, and has the stones to tell you when you need to take a breath.

It doesn't help if you are naturally stubborn, and believe that admitting you're human is a sign of weakness. Can you imagine someone breaking a leg and then still trying to run a marathon? 'It's nothing – just a scratch,' etc. That's nuts, right? So is struggling on past the point of exhaustion. It also doesn't help if you believe that you're there to lift the veil of ignorance from the poor children, and that once they see how much you care about them they'll all adore you for your love and thoughtfulness. They won't. They'll think you're a soft touch. Remember that you need to get the behaviour under control before you bring out the sweetness and light. So don't dash your enthusiasm against their stony indifference. Accept it's going to take time to get them onside, and plan for them to wriggle a bit. Maybe a lot; so don't be Superman/woman. When it gets tough, ask for help. When you need to take a break, make it easier for yourself. Here's how:

◆ **Tell someone that you're struggling**. They may not know. They might think you're absolutely fine until you point out you're drowning. Your mentor, line manager and pastoral buddy – these people should be there for you.

◆ **Cut yourself some slack**. If planning is getting on top of you, then plan for a few easier lessons. An assessment gives you a lesson of monitoring (yes, and more marking, I know). A film can be a valuable educational experience *if* you put it in context and get them to watch out for a few learning points. You could get them to review it, or feed back to the class. Making posters, preparing role plays, or getting a presentation/speeches ready are all valid teaching and learning activities. So is research, project work on computers and reading texts. Whisper it, but the odd worksheet/factsheet lesson will not cause the sky to fall. If it gives you a moment to breathe, and if there is educational value in it, then it's OK to do it. Tell them I said it was OK.

◆ **Cut yourself some slack part two**. If the marking's getting too much for you, examine how much homework you're setting. It is impossible to expect you to mark every book every week in a thorough manner. Sorry, that's just crazy. It takes me an hour and a half to close mark a class, and if I have ten/fifteen different classes then I'm somehow supposed to pull 20 hours out of my socks on top of my school week? Ha-ha-ha, I don't think so, and neither should you. Neither should your line manager or school. Even if you are expected to mark every week, some weeks you can get by 'flicking and ticking' to show that you have seen they are working, and only make the occasional comment when drastic improvement is needed. My aim is thoroughly to mark each book once a month, but at least visit it a couple of times more a month. Don't set long involved essays every week. Get them to peer mark sometimes. Or set homework that doesn't require you sitting at home until two in the morning, like 'learn how to spell five words' or 'find a story from the news that you can discuss.' There are loads of easy marking options that you can employ.

♦ **Cut yourself some slack part three.** Are you doing too much on an extra-curricular basis? Have you picked up clubs, choirs and duties above and beyond expectations? That's great – but remember you're a teacher first and the chess coordinator second. If you can't fit them all in comfortably, drop the chess club. You can still do it once you've earned your teaching chops.

To stay sane make sure that you leave as much school at school as possible; the temptation to take it all home smells delicious, but is ultimately bitter. Clear some space in your head for your friends, your relationships, spouses, children (God, how do you cope? I salute you), hobbies and interests, and in your weekend. For God's sake, keep at least one whole day when you do *nothing* for school. Saturday is a lovely one. Sunday brings with it the familiar evening dread of impending return, so it's harder to keep totally free.

Something you might have to work hard at is to keep your non-teaching friends. Seriously, some people find this really hard, and sink into the school sandpit whole, until people just refer to them as 'Jennifer that became a teacher.' Think of them; contact them; arrange to meet them. I can't tell you how valuable it is to speak to people who aren't teachers, because they can help keep all your stress and worries in perspective. When you're foaming at the mouth because you haven't marked everyone's books over the weekends, they'll be the ones saying, 'Hmm ... have a cocktail and come dancing. Why are you freaking out over a pile of books?'

Seriously, why are you? It is so easy to lose perspective in the enormous ocean of teaching. It feels like nothing else matters. Be clear on this: teaching is an enormous responsibility, and you have a small but tremendously significant part to play in the lives of hundreds of people. But individually, all the many tasks you will face at school are, by themselves, not vital. Very few things will be. That individual book, that individual lesson, that individual task are only part of a greater organism, as we all are in school. So if one thing slides by, if a deadline flies past you making a whooshing noise as it does so, if a set of books remains unmarked for a few weeks, then the sun will stay in the sky, and the dead will remain in their graves.

The most useless advice to give anyone who is stressed is to relax (like saying 'calm down' to an angry man), but seriously: relax. You'll get there. Look after yourself, and treat yourself. Now come here and give me a hug, you big goof![11]

At the start of the third and final term, an unusual hush had descended on some of the Year 11s; they had either smelt the coffee that was imminently about to come scalding down their backs, or they had decided that there was no such thing as coffee, and it didn't matter anyway because they'd have loads of coffee if they wanted, which they didn't, and are you looking at me, mate? Some of the kids displayed levels of keen that I thought only existed in private schools; they asked for after-school revision classes, notes, revision guides, exam tips and so on. It was as if a veil had lifted from them, and some of the most surprising candidates wanted to know how to pass the exams in detail. Having essentially studied the GCSE course along with them as I taught, I was none the wiser, but it was sweet of them to think that I, as a teacher, might know something about what I was talking about.[12]

On the last day of school for Year 11, I cut them some slack and gave them what I thought was a 'fun' lesson – a wordsearch containing key words that could come up in the exam. They looked at me as if I'd just handed them a bag of steaming horse manure.

'Can we just have a free lesson?' they asked.

In another example of how American schools (hey!) always look much more exciting than British schools (oi!) there was an end-of-school celebration night in the local town hall where all the students got dressed up and partied as hard as a dry bar allowed. Only instead of calling it a Prom, we called it an NRA evening.[13] We were all invited to attend, and when I did I was glad I had. Everyone there looked like young adults, so groomed, so human, that it made me see them in a different light.

The last week was a blur; even with half the school missing, that still left a herd to be taught, soothed and entertained as the days got hotter and the school stayed a Victorian sweat box. The syllabus neared the edge of a cliff, and their assessments were largely done, if not marked. I promised to get them back to them at the start of the new school year, and they promised to try to give a sh*t. The pressure to cry havoc and let slip the DVDs was mounting; some of them practically unionized to demand that normal lessons be suspended while we devolved to sessions full of movies and games. I learned an awful lot about the filmic tastes of the average kid

---

[11] Seriously. Come here.

[12] I referred them to the Head of the Department. I didn't just laugh at them or anything.

[13] National Recognition of Achievement, not National Rifle Association. Which would have at least been interesting.

that week. I learned, for instance, that in the lower years, i.e. seven or eight, you could still get away with a sweet movie loosely aimed at children, such as Harry Potter, Mathilda or Babe. The exception was of course my form group, who had it been available, would have asked for Saw; the nearest I had was Big Momma's House 2. Evidently they liked their humour unsophisticated and their sticks squarely slapped. In the upper years, though, if it didn't have a gangster theme, and wasn't populated by hard-talking streetwise teenagers facing drug problems and shooting each other, then I might as well have put Ceebeebies on. It was a struggle. Mind you, at least I gave them something educational: I covered one class who were watching The Fast and the Furious 2 – shoot the bitch.[14] For those of you unfamiliar with the stolen fast car gangster/pole dancing/pimps and bitches world of racing porn, it's ... well, it's exactly as you imagine. All prudes precede their statements with 'I'm not a prude,' so I won't bother. What I did do was shut it down after the third hooker got pistol whipped while naked and being called a 'f**cking b**ch'. The class howled as I tutted. But we ended the lesson on a nice game of hangman, which at least had a suitably gory theme. Ah, they blow up so fast.

Pastoral duties

I've already spoken about your duties towards the students in terms of child protection. Your duties extend far, far beyond that range, thankfully. Like it or not, you have a duty of care to them. Actually, this shouldn't be too dreadful for anyone to realize. After all, teaching is a profession where you deal with young people; it's not lecturing to businessmen, it's a 'working with children' job. If you've volunteered for it (and I understand that at some point your consent is required) then you must have been aware of it. Please try not to enter teaching simply because you, for instance, love your subject but don't like kids. That's a ten car pile-up waiting to happen.

You are, of course, an adult in the lives of children. You already are responsible for them and for their well being in a much broader sense than simply that of your duty towards them as a facilitator of learning. You're going to be a role model for them, because they will unconsciously watch and observe how you act, how you talk, how you move and how you seem to think. Your conduct will be judged and assimilated invisibly, because that's what children do: they watch and observe. This isn't a direct, obvious or necessary process;

---

[14] That might not have been the real title; but it should have been.

they may not imitate you or emulate you. They may not even like the way you do things, but unconsciously you will become part of their understanding of what it means to be an adult. You don't have a choice whether this process happens or not. The only choice you have is: do you want to be a good influence or a bad one?

How do you become a good influence? There are loads of options: for a start, be punctual, civil, kind and positive. This doesn't mean you have to be a snivelling hippie, bending over backwards to meet their whims; you can still be strong, just and decisive – in fact, please do. But it means that gradually they will see that you are well-mannered and respectful in your dealings with them, and they can see how it's done. Some of the pupils you teach may never experience a good role model in their lives, so shudder as you consider that you might be the best one they've got.

There is no statutory requirement for a trainee teacher to become a form tutor in their qualifying year, so you may never experience these delights. If the school is well managed and you're not dissolving in behaviour problems, then this can be a useful thing to start doing; you begin learning how to act in an explicitly pastoral way. It can be tough, though, and if you're feeling the strain of your NQT year, then given the chance, let it go. You can always start doing it next year.

Being a form tutor means that you have to see you class as *your* class, and not just a collection of students that carousel from your hands to the next. Other teachers will look to you for support and guidance, commendations and condemnations. It's in your interests to get to know them as quickly as possible, and find out from the Head of Year about their backgrounds, previous levels and other issues. If your school has a good data system, you might be able to call this up easily. Otherwise you'll need to put some old-fashioned spadework into finding out who your class are. May I suggest talking to them? Your role often involves you acting as the liaison between parent and school, so you should do your best to get to know them as well. My advice is, as soon as you get a form class, put the effort in and call every single parent/guardian on the list, just to introduce yourself. It's time-consuming, but worth a million bucks in building up relationships. Tell them how much you're looking forward to looking after Sonia/James/Sunita. That way, if you do have any naughty calls to make, they'll be far more receptive to hearing from you. Otherwise you're just 'that teacher who calls whenever Sammy bullies someone.'

You need to set a good example with your form class. From you, they will take their cues about the school; if you look like you don't care, they won't either – they're not being paid to. Check them for uniform, for proper equipment, for homework diaries, for anything you can that will instil in them a sense of routine and discipline. It's significant, even if it seems like small stuff to sweat over. Things like that are the poles that hold the circus tent up. If we care about the details then the big picture will take shape. Yes, I know it sounds like a charter for pedantry and obsessive-compulsiveness. It's also a recipe for looking after them; they need the security of knowing what your rules are, even if they resent them. That's how you build up trust, and you'll need it to run a class. More importantly, they'll need it if they want to feel safe, looked after and secure. They are, after all, children. Look after them with your conduct, how you speak and how you treat them. Never forget that your position isn't simply one of walking into a room, talking about geography a bit and walking out to applause. You're training them to be an adult, whether you want to or not. You are. So take this part of your job seriously.

We ended on a whole school assembly where the Head handed out certificates for perfect attendance and punctuality, surely the least sought-after accolade in the teenage community, unless you're a white rabbit. We all stood on the edges and frowned intensely at our students who were wriggling with unconcealed, furious antipathy. They only gathered focus again when members of the school body got up to murder popular contemporary pop tunes, accompanied by an earnest music teacher who rescued the melody. There were about three or four criminal performances that the kids lapped up like custard (usually because the performers were hard girls who courted popularity or notoriety) and then one knockout, stand-up song by a nervy looking elf from Year seven who would blow the roof off. The Head Teacher gave a farewell speech to say how proud he was to be part of the school community, and then everyone went home, apart from us, because we all went back to the school, heard a few tearful farewell speeches from leaving colleagues, and then went over the road to the pub to get smashed in the afternoon.

It may not have been elegant, but at least there was the sense of ceremony. The year was over. Two hundred days of teaching, counted down, column and row, in digits scratched on a jail cell wall. Two hundred days. On reality shows it's become fashionable to say that you've been on a journey, normally because the participants can't think of anything more meaningful to describe, and the journey has become the accepted idiom to represent 'I'm slightly illiterate but I want to express a continuum of experiences that I have found meaningful.'

It was a journey.

Being social

I've talked a lot about maintaining a teacher persona and being professional at all times. There will also be times throughout even your first year when you may be called on to accompany the students on more social situations, such as trips. In these situations it is essential that you remain 'on the job' because the kids need you to be a grown-up, not a cheeky chappy. But there are other times too when you might allow yourself to smile a little because the situation demands it. If there is an end of school party, for example, I recommend you go to it, and stand on the edges bobbing slowly if any music plays, or applauding with pride whenever a student takes to the stage to murder 'Unfaithful' or anything by Akon. If there is a prize-giving evening, or a school show, or a talent night, or a play, then go. Go, go, go. You will see the students trying their hardest, dressing up, pretending to be grown-ups, and feeling just as awkward and excited as you did when you were their age. It is, in my experience, a joy to behold. The pupils may even speak to you like a human being, and they will certainly appreciate you being there, even if they keep it well hidden.

They are all human; they are all children, even the odd ones. And they instinctively want to share their experiences with other people. Without suggesting that you take to the dance floor and bust some phat moves with them, get involved. In some ways it can be seen as a reward for the hard work you've put in with them, and if you have any kind of heart at all you'll feel a glow of pride at the same time as they do. School plays and shows are enjoyed by three groups of people: the kids, their families and you. Trust me on this one.

It also gives you something to talk to them about in form time ...

Of course, being social usually means with your peers and colleagues; throughout the year you will be invited, informally or formally, to staff functions and engagements, from pints in the pub with your department to the staff party. As far as you are able, and remembering your work/life balance, I would suggest that in your first year it is important – actually important – to go to as many of these as possible. If you've been invited out, then accept the kindness. Schools can be lonely places, and you'll need every friend you can get. You never know, you might strike up friendships across the most unlikely of divides, and it's a great leveller to be dancing, drinking, karaoke-ing or just out with your colleagues.[15] Some of them will

---

[15] If you haven't worked it out already, I am unspeakably vulgar.

make your skin crawl – fine; you've found something out. Some of them will resonate with you, and you'll make friends. Do it, because being a team is what makes us stronger than any number of noisy, noisesome children. And you'll have some fun. As long as your idea of fun involves talking to teachers, that is ...

10 | The plenary: *What have we learned?*

We are reliably informed that every lesson should end with a plenary, so I think this book should, too. Given that books are still (unless Steve Jobs and Bill Gates have pulled a rabbit out of a hat since I wrote this) a one-way process, I'm going to find it very hard to see you all if I ask you to put your hands up, or traffic light your understanding. Which means I'll finish on a summary of what has gone before in case I haven't made it clear enough already. Which is very possible.

What could be done better next time?

Looking back on my own experiences of teacher training, I realized that there was so much that could have been done differently in order to make the training experience better. This is the nature of life – often we don't understand an opportunity until it sails past us; often we only truly learn long after an event, and we can blend our experiences with perspective, time and reflection. This is, I think, the way of things, and regret can often be a useless sentiment. But it can serve to sharpen one's resolve not to repeat mistakes made, and that has been one of the aims of this book. As I have mentioned many times, experience and learning often cannot happen simply by mere rumination: many things can only be properly learned when they have been experienced and practised, like riding a bicycle. But learning can be accelerated if the learning is given a context, and if the time spent reflecting on it is guided by the experiences of others. To continue the tired old bicycle metaphor, riding a bike might be a skill best learned through practice, but it doesn't hurt if someone tells you to press the brakes and not the bell when you want to stop.

There are enormous problems in the British teacher training cycle. I say this not to carp or snipe, but because I think every teacher trainee needs to understand that the system isn't perfect (what system is?) and that it would be opportune to make the most of the experience, and develop strategies to make the experience as useful as possible. For example, one of my most astonishing observations was that teacher training in the UK does not contain anything like the behaviour management preparation that the modern teacher requires. There still seems to be an assumption that teachers will, by and large, walk into schools where classroom compliance will be attained relatively easily. This, of course, is the raving of a lunatic. Bad behaviour is widespread. Teacher training is based on an outdated paradigm. One reason for this is to do with human nature, and the nature of memory. Even in the schools I have worked in, I have seen spectacular refusals to acknowledge the misbehaviour around us. Here's why:

♦ Many of the people involved in senior management/teacher training are highly experienced teachers, for whom bad behaviour is something they encounter on an infrequent basis. For this reason, it becomes easy to assume that bad behaviour either doesn't exist, or 'isn't that bad'. Well, it is if you're a new teacher.

♦ Many of these people enjoy high status in schools, which often provides a force field of invincibility – it takes a particularly hard kid to go toe to toe with the Head Master, for instance, when even the cheekiest young scamp knows he can have him out on his ear before lunch time.

♦ Many of these people don't actually teach that much any more; or if they do, they teach sixth form or small classes. In some cases, they may still teach the odd challenging group, but with plenty of preparation and reflection time between lessons they find it easier to deal with the occasional problem.

♦ In many situations, some of these people haven't stepped into a classroom for some years. It's easy to forget how awful it can be to be new. Challenging kids save their very worst behaviour for new teachers, uncertain in their powers and skills.

♦ Some of these people then develop the rather tasteless opinion that bad behaviour is 'the fault' of the teacher, something that makes me want to tear someone's head off in philosophical revulsion. If a kid decides to pour Tippex into someone's bag, only the maddest of the mad would say it was the teacher who did it. Trust me, I teach ethics; there's not a definition of responsibility in the world you could use to shoehorn blame on to the teacher. Sure, the kids will respond better if the teacher acts in certain ways, but as long as we choose to believe in the concept of freewill (and I do) then we have to assume that children aren't mindless robots, guided on programs of self-destruction unless we intervene.

Such people usually decide that the teacher needs 'support' which usually takes the form of being made to feel like a useless teacher. Let me be clear abut this: if a kid misbehaves in a classroom, it's the kid that should spend some time in the Big House, not the Teacher. Any school that doesn't back its teachers by default against the kids in behaviour issues, doesn't deserve to have any.

You might be lucky and get a school placement in a challenging situation but have an inspiring behaviour expert to guide you who you can emulate. But just as likely, you might not. You might, like me, get a fairly patchy introduction to the skills of behaviour management. And as I mentioned earlier, I don't blame the schools or the teachers involved for this situation. They haven't been trained to teach teachers. They don't get paid extra. They still have busy working lives themselves. But the school placement system is an enormously hit-and-miss affair, where if you get great training, it's accidental.

But until things change, that's what we work with. So it's up to you as a trainee to make the most of it. You cannot be a passive recipient of education (which funnily enough, is exactly what we say to the kids); you have to grab it by the throat and say, 'what can you teach me?' Do the reading. Write up your reflections. Ask questions. Do observations. Ask for help. Demand to be observed if you want advice on something. It's a training process where you have to be an adult, and if you're not comfortable with that, then you're going to have to learn.

Being a professional

One of the themes I often return to is the idea that teaching is a profession; by that I mean it is more than a collection of facts and figures, it is a collection of skills and judgements. Aristotle would call the skill you need *nous*, which means wisdom, but also means the ability to weigh things up, assess, decide and adjudicate, depending on individual situations. Doctors and lawyers need *nous*, because no matter how much you learn you'll always have to apply what you've learned in a different way depending on the situation. Sometimes you have to make a best guess. Sometimes you have to use your intuition.

Teaching is also a job where you can't prescribe a rule for every situation. This is at odds with the nature of bureaucracy; over the past few decades there has been an increasing tendency to develop rules and guidelines for teachers, 'best practice' and 'recommendations' that sound like suggestions but are really coded instructions, that you ignore at your peril. This isn't a controversial observation; this is a shift in the way the profession is treated. Especially since the Education Reform Act 1988 onwards, control over education has originated all the way back to cabinet level and beyond, often directly from the Prime Minister himself. Even Education ministers themselves have been routinely sidelined in favour of direct instruction from Number Ten. The net result of this is that the profession has never been more encumbered with rules and regulations about how to teach. Teachers are not only told what to teach, but how to teach.

I could write a book about the dubiousness of the direction from the DfE, and the suspiciously fishy provenance of the motivation behind it (and I probably will), but for now it is enough to say that you will be told many, many things on your training and by others about the 'best way' to teach. I can assure you of this one thing, which is endlessly worth repeating: no one *knows* anything. No method of teaching has been exhaustively proven to be superior to another, universally and for all children in all circumstances. I guarantee it. So learn what you think is the best way to teach. Of course, be aware of what will be required of you as an employee in a state institution, and be prepared to deliver what is required of you for employment purposes. But try to keep you head above the water and see clearly. You are, believe it or not, a professional, not a delivery mechanism for a set of instructions and skill sets: a professional. So be one.

Looking beyond your first year

Let me extend hypothetical congratulations on the completion of your hypothetical training year. At the end of this process, the member of staff responsible for certifying NQTs will at some point sit down with you and establish if you have met the criteria for certification. Or, if the school has problems putting its socks on the right way, you might just get a letter in your pigeonhole saying 'Well done, you're in,' or something similar. Of course, it might not have gone so well for you; if your observations haven't been so smooth, and if the kids still stand in your classes and pretend to be on strike, you might have some problems. The school is not required to certify you, nor is the process automatic. However, if I can offer some reassurance, the school needs to be very careful before it refuses to pass you. For example, it must have given you a long period of notice to indicate that you possibly might not get through the process; furthermore, it needs to show an enormous amount of evidence to prove that it has tried to avoid you failing the induction year, for example, by providing extra training, plenty of paired observations, time off to plan and learn, etc. Given that refusing to certify you will mean that they can't employ you as a teacher, they will (or should) move mountains to avoid this. And they will certainly have involved the LEA by this point. If the worst happens and you fail the induction year, you can still try again in another school.

If you have managed to finish the year and get the stamp of approval, what are your next steps?

Moving on

When you are a newly qualified teacher, options start to open up to you like flowers. You may dream of promotion. If so, well done, you ambitious little scamp. Be careful though – are you ready for promotion? Some schools are forced to promote extremely green staff into positions they aren't ready for. Sometimes it's wiser to forgo the quick buck and focus on developing yourself as a teacher.[1]

There are a huge number of extra responsibilities that you can go for in schools – it's one of the reasons they're such interesting places to work. After a year in a school you will have started to realize what kind of teaching interests you, so you can aim to work more in those areas: gifted and talented, SEN, clubs, drama, pastoral support, behaviour management; go crazy. Working in these roles doesn't always mean getting paid; often you might just want to offer your services to the people in charge of these areas, and learn from them for free. It's not exploitation if you're getting something useful out of it. Teaching is also a brilliant profession because you can do things because you enjoy it, not just because you get paid to do it. That's the kind of people we are, and that's how we roll.

Or there might be an actual post up for offer: great – if you feel ready for it, go for it, and the interviewing panel will tell you if you're

---

[1] Yeah I know; I can stick it up my backside, can't I? Gimme, gimme, gimme.

ready for it too. If you don't get the first post you apply for, for God's sake be grown up and don't sulk. Meet defeat with the same magnanimity you meet success, and you will gain the admiration of your peers and line management. And don't just quit in a fit of pique.

Quitting

Perhaps you have decided that your school and you aren't compatible life partners. There are pluses and minuses to leaving after your NQT year. It's a good idea if you just know that you're not going to work out in the school – it might be too badly behaved, or too well behaved, or you might totally disagree with the school ethos, whatever. In that case, it might be best for you to move on; nobody but you will make yourself happier. But be careful; if you stay on at your first-year school, you will reap the benefits of a developing relationship with the children you have already taught; you will be a known face, and even the kids you don't teach will start to recognize you as an authority. Behaviour management famously gets easier as time goes by, if you keep applying the rules I have mentioned. If you go somewhere new then you start from square one, building up the relationships, albeit with a better grasp of the things you have to do. Even very experienced teachers experience difficulties when they go to new schools; it's just that, for them, they get the machinery started much more quickly so that the kids respect them in a fraction of the time it would normally take.

But changing schools can be a great thing to do if an opportunity comes up in the type of school you really see yourself in; if the management shares your vision for education, or if it's simply a case of geographical proximity to your home. I would counsel anyone almost never to leave a school in their induction year, simply because it's much harder to start up a new year somewhere else than it is to finish a tough one. But once you've finished the induction year, the education world is your oyster.

Staying

Or don't quit. You never really achieve the status of perfect teacher; you merely keep developing. Unfortunately many teachers don't keep developing; they get to a certain plateau of ability, behaviour and subject knowledge, and sort of … settle. It's as if they've decided they're comfortable, and this will do nicely, thanks. Ironically, such teachers can often experience high levels of job dissatisfaction, poor behaviour and minimal promotion. But as I've said, humans will do a lot more to avoid immediate discomfort rather than pursue distant gain. I urge you not to 'settle'. Keep pushing yourself as a teacher; keep learning, keep trying to get better. Put yourself in situations you're not used to; learn new skills; observe other people. You can only improve. And not only that but you will enjoy yourself much, much more. You are a human being, infinitely flexible and adaptable, with seemingly limitless potential to learn and grow. Imagine what you can become if you try – not a superhuman, but a constantly improving version of yourself. Imagine flourishing every year, achieving new and greater things every season. Imagine what you could do for the kids. Imagine what you can do for yourself. That's why you should never quit. In fact, once a few years have passed, it's often a good idea to change schools, just to see how other people do it. It's drastic, but something you should consider.

But such considerations are far, far beyond the scope of this book. Your first, last and everything[2] goal right now is to get the skills necessary to become the best teacher you can be. I hope that by guiding you through my experiences I have helped to point out some of the bear traps and spike pits that wait for the earnest but foolish teacher. You will make many mistakes of your own, but that will always be the best way to learn. If I have suggested how to improve the quality of your mistakes, then I am a happy man. Teaching is the best job in the world, as I see it. Nowhere else do you get the chance to help so many people improve the quality of their lives. It's partly missionary work, partly charity work and all hard work. That's why it's the best job in the world. You will never have a dull day because the children won't let you. You might have lots of extremely difficult days, but when was anything worthwhile ever achieved without a bit of sweat?

I've tried to paint an unromantic picture of teaching; I've tried to portray it in its underwear because I don't think that a cosy, rosy manual about teacher training is either honest or useful to you. But the reason I have done so isn't to put people off; it's to encourage them. Teaching is an absolute hoot, and I have never been happier in my life than since I started, despite what my early chapters may have indicated.

Learning how to scale the infinitely variable peaks of the teacher's mountain range has proven to be worth countless blessings to me,

---

[2] © Barry White.

Appendix: Useful websites

These are some suggestions about where you can find out more about the technical aspects of becoming a teacher; they explain the process in much more and better detail than I can, which is why this book points to them rather than attempts to reproduce the same information.

The Training and Development Agency for Schools (TDA) is the 'national agency and recognized body responsible for the training and development of the school workforce'. Find them at http://www.tda.gov.uk. This is a fabulously well-designed and informative portal, so spend a lot of time on it. Aimed at prospective teachers in England and Wales. In 2012 this organization's role is absorbed into the DfE.

Want to become a McTeacher? Go to http://www.teachinginscotland.com to find out about training with a whisky flavour. Or try http://www.deni.gov.uk/index/teachers-pg/teachers-teachinginnorthernireland_pg.htm if you're in Northern Ireland.

If you're interested in training via the SCITT route (School-Centred Initial Teacher Training), then go to http://www.tda.gov.uk/Recruit/thetrainingprocess/trainingproviders/scittproviders.aspx to find out more, and to get an up-to-date list of providers.

If you want to teach in a Catholic school, you're advised to check out http://www.brs-ccrs.org.uk/, which is the site of the Board of Religious Studies. It offers advice and training so that you don't get Rosemary and your Rosary mixed up.

http://www.teachfirst.org.uk/ is the address of Teach First, the independent charity set up by businesses to sponsor and promote highly qualified applicants from other sectors.

http://community.tes.co.uk/forums/5.aspx is the behaviour forum in which I advise, on the excellent TES portal TSLonline. The standard of contributors is usually extremely high. You can also link to dozens of other forums where you can ask questions from a national community of teachers who almost always answer promptly and efficiently.

http://www.tes.co.uk/resourcesHome.aspx?navcode=70 is another part of the TSLonline portal, where new (and old) teachers can access thousands of individual resources to use in their lessons: lesson plans, activities, ideas, work sheets and more. Invaluable. And free.

If you like reading interesting, blunt commentary on the state of modern education, I wholeheartedly endorse this blog: http://teachingbattleground.wordpress.com/, written by one of the best education bloggers in the UK, oldandrew. Brilliant, and spot on. I could also mention my own blog, http://behaviourguru.blogspot.com/ which is the home of my own personal take on our noble and surreal profession.

http://www.education.gov.uk/. This is the official Department for Education website, where you can keep up to date with the latest initiatives before the next Cabinet Musical Chairs, and the latest minister pulls something new out of their hat. Still, important to know what you'll be asked to do in eighteen months' time.

http://www.teachernet.gov.uk/. This is the DfE link for teachers (or 'schools workforce' as they horrifyingly put it. My blood curdles). Very useful for articles, official guidelines and 'best practice'; if you want a piece of educational slang deciphered or explained then this is the place for you, especially if you like pages and pages of lethargic text written in the passive tense.

http://www.bbc.co.uk/news/education/. The good old BBC. Still worth every penny of a licence fee, and its continuing coverage of educational news is just one reason why.

Index